Rip the Page!

Rip the Page!

Adventures in Creative Writing

Karen Benke

ROOST
BOOKS

Boston & London
2010

ROOST BOOKS
An imprint of Shambhala Publications, Inc.
Horticultural Hall
300 Massachusetts Avenue
Boston, Massachusetts 02115
roostbooks.com

9 8 7 6 5

Printed in the United States of America

♾ This edition is printed on acid-free paper that meets the
American National Standards Institute Z39.48 Standard.
♻ Shambhala Publications makes every effort to print
on recycled paper. For more information please visit
www.shambhala.com.

Distributed in the United States by Random House, Inc.,
and in Canada by Random House of Canada Ltd

Designed by Lora Zorian

LIBRARY OF CONGRESS CATALOGING-IN-PUBLICATION DATA

Benke, Karen.
Rip the page!: adventures in creative writing / Karen Benke.—1st ed.
p.   cm.
Includes index.
ISBN 978-1-59030-812-7 (pbk.: alk. paper)
1. Creative writing. 2. Authorship. 3. English language—Rhetoric.
4. English language Composition and exercises. I. Title.
PE1404.B45 2010
808'.042—dc22
2010008803

For all the young and young-at-heart creative writers.
And for Collin Prell, my bright-eyed Muse.

"There is no use trying," said Alice; "one *can't* believe impossible things."

"I dare say you haven't had much practice," said the Queen. "When I was your age, I always did it for half an hour a day. Why, sometimes I've believed as many as six impossible things before breakfast."

—Lewis Carroll, *Through the Looking Glass*

CONTENTS

INTRODUCTION

Dear Fellow Adventurer,

Relax. This book isn't about assignments or homework or worksheets. This book is a not-so-secret combustible collection of ideas to excite and encourage the creative writer in you. It's a book for you to write in, explore, share, and rip— that's right, you get to tear pages right out of this book! (But only if it's *your* book.)

In the next 230 pages, you'll find Word Lists to help you when your writing is stuck, Try This experiments to spark new ideas, Suddenly a Story . . . pieces to inspire you to collect and pay attention to truths *and* lies, Definition Decoders to deepen your writing knowledge, and Notes from real-life writers who will share their thoughts on what it takes to put your voice on the page.

Of course, with all these sections you can still use this book any way that you want. *You* decide if you open to the last page first or begin someplace deep in the middle. If you don't like what's on page 62, skip it. (Page 62 gave me problems, too.) If you like something, put stars around it. If you don't like something, cross it out. This is your book to read, hug, take for a walk, snack on, laugh with, even kiss. You decide what, when, how, where, why, and why not. There's no wrong or right way to write creatively. Really. There's just *your* way. The only thing this book needs is *your* imagination for the journey. Write what *you* and no one else in the world can. Break rules. Take risks. Talk back. Make "mistakes." Give yourself miles of time and plenty of space. Let the tip of your pen scrawl, scribble, leap, doodle, and *rip, rip, rip*! That's what creative writers do when they aren't busy staring, day-dreaming, and eavesdropping.

Once you get going, maybe you'll share something you write with me. (Maybe I'll write you back.) Remember: when you trust your words to the page, you're braver than you think.

Your Friend,

Karen

What Can You Write With?

Forget the usual suspects: pencils, pens, paint, chalk, Sharpie markers, purple crayons . . .What if you could write with *anything* today? What if you could wedge between the fingers of your left or right hand, a memory? Your infinite imagination? The power of creativity? A spinning planet? The state of forgiveness? A tree trunk, or a ray of sunlight? Well, guess what? In the realm of creative writing, you can. There are trillions of possibilities, and they keep on expanding into endless whirling patterns. What can you add to the things *you* can write with today?

What I Write With

I can write with the tainted light of tattered forgiveness
I can write with the smallest stars of the almost-not-seen
I can write with the long sticky threads of sacred spider webs
I can write with the spinning planets of darkness and danger
I can write with my unseen, dazzling trick-up-my-sleeve schemes

Your Turn

I can write with

_____

I can write with

_____

I can write with

_____

I can write with

_____

I can write with

_____

I can write with

_____

I can write with

_____

I can write with

_____

Favorite Words

A creative writer's imagination is hungry for words. To keep up your creative energy, you must feed your imagination 24 times or more each day (and night). Here's a list of some of my favorite words to snack on. Help yourself. Graze. Trade. Visit this page *whenever* your imagination starts to growl and needs to nibble. What are some of your favorite 1, 2, 3, 4 syllable words to taste today?

smuggle	unicycle	baffle	polliwog
traverse	soprano	spool	juggle
goblet	honeysuckle	wizard	passage
tackle	kettle	cicada	kimono
periwinkle	gopher	migration	tackle
spiral	prairie	gargoyle	vermillion
hibernate	knot-hole	cobbler	sleuth
Wednesday	souvenir	hubcap	glockenspiel
glacier	hatch	barrette	droplet
avalanche	zipper	pendulum	catacomb
sandwich	crackle	froth	dollop
falafel	scroll	eddies	chipper
locket	snippet	apostrophe	dapple
flutter	snuggle	makeshift	lickety-split
snorkel	totem	centipede	question mark

Try This....

Questions to Ask Yourself

What if the next question you asked could take you to a part of your mind where you've never been before? What if just by posing a question, or imagining how you'd answer it, you could dream deeper, think wider, imagine taller, wish farther? Here are 26 questions to answer any way you please. These aren't trick questions; just questions that need a different kind of attention as you play with discovering *your* answers. Your answers can be true *and* false, long *and* short, fast *and* slow, soft *and* chewy. Take a walk on the near *and* far side of your life. There's no wrong path. Whatever's in your mind is fine. Discover how curious, gentle, kind, funny, snotty, honest, contagious, and outrageous you can be as you take your trip one word-step at a time into the mapless unknown.

Hints:

Anything you write is right.

Don't worry about spelling or pretty, perfect letters.

Make sense, or not. Experiment.

Why not answer a question with a question?

Your Turn

Play with all your options and see where your answers lead. If your words need more room, let them wander down, across, up, and over the edges of the page.

Unleash your wildest, most untamed dream. Where does it want to run?

Mine starts to kick & buck & heads straight for the open gate, out across the far field, up into...

If you plant your heart, what might grow? What color are its shoes?

If you stand on your hands, where will you walk; how will you fall? Who's going with you?

If you peek under the tent of life, what do you hear? What do you see? What makes you sneeze?

What are the names of your fingers? toes? each hand and foot? your nose?

What do you most love to count? What can't be counted?

Where did you find your silliest song? your deepest calm? your good luck charm?

Why don't you ever run out of surprises? Who is your supplier?

——— — — —— — —— — —— — —— ——— — — —— — —— — ——

What do you love at the bottom? What do you fear at the top?

——— — — —— — —— — —— — —— ——— — — —— — —— — ——

Where do you most like to fly? What do your wings look like today?

——— — — —— — —— — —— — —— ——— — — —— — —— — ——

What's your favorite memory trapped under? Where is it going next?

——— — — —— — —— — —— — —— ——— — — —— — —— — ——

What natural disaster would you most like to be caught in if you wouldn't be hurt?

——— — — —— — —— — —— — —— ——— — — —— — —— — ——

You get to grant someone a wish—who is the person? What is the wish?

——— — — —— — —— — —— — —— ——— — — —— — —— — ——

If you could disappear into one color for a day, what color? What day?

——— — — —— — —— — —— — —— ——— — — —— — —— — ——

Rip the Page!

Write 100 words (or more) as one *looooong* word withoutanyspacesinbetween, around the edge of this page . . . don't stop until you've made a spiral in the center. Use it to hypnotize your hamster, dog, sister, brother, mother, or father as you slowly whisper, "You're getting sleepy . . . very, very sleepy." Say the long spiraled word you've created 3 times. This will give your mouth, jaw, tongue, cheeks, and any loose teeth a workout. You can try hypnotizing your cat, but chances are he's already sleeping.

Yellow Car

Last week, a boy I know was in the car with his mom, riding to school, the store, the library, back home—all the places they go— when he noticed there weren't any yellow cars on the road.

"Where are all the yellow cars?" he asked. His mom reminded him about taxis and asked if he was feeling OK.

And that's when he told her he was going to count *every* speck of yellow he could find. Almost immediately, he started seeing yellow *everywhere:* the double lines of crosswalks; the eyes of a black cat, a man in a rain slicker, walking a yellow Lab; fire hydrants; caution signs; a row of sunflowers peeking over a fence. And yellow cars—*everywhere!* Trucks and buses and bicycles too. What if *whatever* you put your attention on creates what you see? What if, today yellow cars . . . what if tomorrow, world peace?

What's something you hardly notice, wonder about, wish you could find or see? A stunt plane in a nosedive? A colony of caterpillars? Maybe an old friend from second grade? Jot down a few (or a few hundred) of these *somethings,* and in the shape of an *X*-marks-the-spot, include a detail about where you found one thing on your list and what you plan to find next.

⑧ Wishes

What if no wish was too big or too small, and *everything* under the moon and beyond the slanted rays of the sun was possible? What if the more you paid attention to a certain wish, the stronger it got? What if all you had to do was close your eyes and pull 8 wishes from deep inside . . . and *whatever* you *truly* longed for began to float a little closer? Why 8? Well, the number 8 is considered extremely lucky. In China, for example, the opening ceremony of the Summer Olympics in Beijing started at 8 seconds and 8 minutes past 8 p.m., local time, on August 8, 2008!

8 Rules For Letting a Wish Come True

1. Wait for a full moon.
2. Make sure what you wish for is what you *really* want.
3. To cancel a wish just make the opposite wish.
4. At first, don't talk about your wish with anyone.
   It might break the spell!
5. Pay attention to your wish every day for 8 days.
   (Sing to it, write it a poem . . .)
6. Act (and feel) as if your wish has *already* come true.
7. Reinvent whatever your life gives you.
8. Smile and thank your wish for revealing itself to you.

Wishing Windowsill

A package arrives without a return address—
Inside I find a note asking me to make a wish.
I unwrap 8 small paintings from red paper:
the first is a tree in winter, with a crow on a branch
looking like he's keeping a secret I need to know.
The second is a house beside a river with a bridge
and a crescent moon asleep in the sideways sky.
The third is blank except for a yellow circle
that I decide is a door to the sun.
The fourth has a gold coin taped to the corner, circa 1929.
The fifth and sixth is a diptych of clouds and mist.
Inspiration is written in cursive on the seventh
with silver sparks flying off each letter's rise and fall.
The eighth painting's happy and reminds me of you, smiling.

—Karen

Your Turn

Dear Writer,

Writing. There's good news and bad news. Here's the good news:

1. If you write, you're a writer.
2. Most of the things that get you in trouble with grown-ups can be used in stories later.
3. Ditto, getting hurt.
4. Spelling has nothing to do with good writing.
5. Reading does.

Here's the bad news:

1. To be a writer, you have to write.

When I was a kid, I didn't really care about writers. Actually, I didn't believe in them. I thought writers were—not superhuman (I wasn't that confused)—but not living on Earth in the same way I was. Books were my own separate world, an unreal place that had nothing to do with my life. It seemed to me that the books I loved must have emanated from people who inhabited a world of equal unreality. Now that I'm a writer myself, I no longer think that writers live in another world. I wish they did. I wish I lived in some magical place where I could produce a book without sitting down and writing the same sentence over and over dozens (or hundreds) of times. But I live here, on Earth, with all the other writers, all of us writing and re-writing and re-writing one more time, trying to make the sentences right. This is the bad news and the good news, too, because it means that anyone who does the work of writing—the intensive, repetitious, often fruitless work of writing—is that otherworldly creature, a writer.

From,

Annie

A Sample of Annie Barrows's Writing

FROM *The Magic Half*

The notebook fell from Miri's hands, and she stared wide-eyed at the white wall before her. It *had* all happened. The magic was real. She had gone back in time that afternoon and met an eleven-year-old girl named Molly. The last tiny doubt disappeared from her mind like a popping soap bubble, and a question arose to fill the newly cleared space: Why? Why had it happened? And why had the magic chosen her?

Miri was pretty sure that it was not because she was good. Cinderella, for example, now *she* was good: singing while she cleaned the house, happily sewing for her nasty stepsisters. And that's why her fairy godmother had given her the coach, the dress, the prince. Miri had always found Cinderella annoying, but she was definitely better than Miri. Miri complained if she had to clean her own room. And look at this afternoon—she had almost killed Ray with a shovel. No, the magic hadn't chosen her because she was good.

When Annie Barrows was a kid, she was always good and sweet and kind and pure of heart. She never did anything bad. Well, except for the thing with the lipstick. And, OK, some people might think what she did to the cat was bad, but the cat didn't mind. The cat liked it. To find out more about the books Annie writes for kids, visit www.anniebarrows.com.

An Attitude of Gratitude

Do you ever go around complaining—OK, maybe even whining—about everything you don't have: a cool-looking *this*; tricked-out *that*; the new, latest, best, most expensive remote-control, super-fast, double-decker, super-sonic *thing-a-ma-jig?* We all do it. But all that wanting (and whining) can get to feeling *sooooo* miserable. There's *got* to be a way to toss all that wanting into reverse, push the pause button, and find the attitude of gratitude lever. So we can at least remember the amazing things we *do* have, but might have forgotten. You know, simple things like our fingers and thumbs that hold pencils and forks and scratch our itchy backs. And what about these amazing imaginations that we were born with and get to keep *expanding*? What about moms and dads, grandmas and grandpas, sisters, brothers, aunts, uncles, cousins, and all our chosen friends? And don't forget about heartbeats and seasons, maple trees and grilled cheese sandwiches. Once you start down this slope, you'll begin noticing an avalanche of all these big and small gifts given especially to *you*. And here's the best-kept secret of all: this attitude of gratitude is the only thing that will ever truly make us feel happy, content, satisfied, or full.

Autumn's Gift

Maples deepen into rusts and plum;
the poplars in the upper boughs go golden.
Grass stiffens with insistent frost; pine needles
from the limbs above lay strewn upon the ground
like a game of pick-up sticks. There's a clean edge to things—
fences, roof lines, ridge. The air is cold.
Suddenly the dog seems older, the children taller.
We pull the collars of our jackets tighter at the neck,
slip our hands inside our sleeves, and go on believing,
as did Penelope, that a world this loved will not vanish.

—Kathy Evans

Your Turn

Try on an attitude of gratitude. What do you thank your lucky stars for?

What You've Never Told Anyone

I've never told anyone that I like to sit in a corner of my backyard and watch the bees enter their hive in the leaning oak while crows land on my roof and scare the squirrels. I've never told anyone I have three false teeth and was once bit by a shark who left a scar that required 45 stitches. . . . that I'm terrified of deep water but love swimming the butterfly stroke, so jump into the sea anyway and let loose a laughing-scream. I've never told anyone that short stories scare me the longest and that last winter I watched a boy feed cracked corn straight from his hand to a family of deer. I've never told anyone that I once pushed a marble up my nose just to see how it would feel and, yes, *I'm* the one who rescued those snails off the sidewalk and set them free in the overgrown ivy. I've never told anyone that the way leaves fall from trees makes me sad and that I want to live in Japan when I'm 93 and learn to perform a tea ceremony. I've never told anyone that I climbed through my skylight last night, to sit on the roof and imagine what I'd look like asleep on the moon.

19

Wade on to the page and mix 6 things you've never told anyone with 6 things that might have nothing to do with you. String together some truthful lies and some lying truths. If you feel shy as you're writing, think of the bravest person you know and finish the sentence you most want to erase. Don't share what you write with anyone (unless you really want to).

Your Turn

Repetition

Purposely putting repetition in your writing adds another layer of fun. "Rose is a rose is a rose is a rose is a rose." Gertrude Stein, a famous poet of the last century, wrote that line of repetition. She also wrote, "To write is to write is to write is to write is to write is to write is to write is to write." Repeated words grab the ears' attention. *Please? Oh, please? Pretty please? Pleeease! Are we almost there? Are we? Are we there yet?* Go on, give it a try. Add repetition to your everyday questions and begging—then find out for yourself how powerful (or annoying) you sound. Pick up a word you like and use it again and again (and again). Then find a poem or story you've already written and figure out 12 places to fit your repeating word. In the poem below, check out the way Paul Hoover put the word "famous" into his poem 12 times. OK, 13, if you count the title.

Here are some other words you might use for purposes of repetition:

a specific number, like *12; 105; 3.7 million . . .*

a color like *brown; gray; flying silver* or *flickering orange . . .*

an adjective like *shining* or *famous* or *twisted* or *secret-coded . . .*

two words like *No way* or *You must* or *Come in!*

Famous

Famous snow falling,
covering a mountain famous for its snow.
Famous cedars leaning in the wind.

A stone is famous at the bottom of the river.
But the river is normal enough.
It goes here to there.

The famous dust is falling,
in nondescript corners and the famous corners, too,
where you stood or I stood

and someone will be standing
for the first time soon. Cup famous for some reason.
Bowl famous to its spoon.

Sunlight famous, most famous of all
as it climbs the garden wall.
Famous moon, coming through night

notorious for its darkness,
and Earth that is famous only on Earth,
with its sweet smell of history.

—Paul Hoover

Before You Start Your Journey

You must walk across the salt flats with pockets full of light. You must see through the blurry air to find your true glow. You must read a story about the past that's as slippery as fish. You must be miles away before you start your journey. You must be aware that when your heart gets crushed, the beat stops. In winter, you must see the snow falling up and down. And later, you must see it melting away, though the cold never stops.

—Patrick

Use repetition for chants and casting spells, too . . .

Waging Peace...
Breath by Breath

You've probably heard, and experienced, that practice makes perfect. Well, what if you practiced being curious about *everything* around you for a few minutes today? Or even for just a minute or two? What have you got to lose? Besides, doesn't the world have enough of that anger and fear stuff already? Luckily, if you're a kid, you laugh around 300–400 times a day. But grown-ups . . . they only laugh about 15 times a day. How sad is that?! What if, magically, there was a way to balance out the situation? What if whatever awful, terrible, no-good thing you *breathed in,* you could instantly transform? Just by *breathing out*? So that by the time you exhaled, that sad, angry, fearful thing was *changed* into something joyful, smiling, and maybe even laughing? A few 11-year-olds tried this as a creative writing experiment. Here's what surprised them as they inhaled and exhaled on the page:

Breathe in nuclear weapons
Breathe out Siberian tigers not going extinct
Breathe in crashing bicycles
Breathe out a new word for happiness
(that'll catch you when you fall)

Breathe in life's dull moments
Breathe out a bubble of soft chewing gum
Breathe in the trouble of war
Breathe out the sweetness of a kept promise
Breathe in the shattering-horrible
Breathe out the precise shade of blue at the beach
Breathe in the fear of thunder
Breathe out the lightning-truth forever within reach.

—Monet and friends

Your Turn

You breathe approximately 18,000–30,000 times per day, in and out, more than 10 million times per year! (That's 20 times per minute.) Can you spare one inhalation and one exhalation to this page?

How Things Began

Do you ever wonder how a certain thing got its start? Like the number 7? Where did he—*she?*—come from? And what about all those squiggly punctuation marks? The resting period, sly comma, excited exclamation point, tired question mark—where did *they* sprout from? A poet named Maurya Simon wrote a book of poems called *A Brief History of Punctuation,* where she imagines the creation of the question mark "grew slowly, atom by atom, carving its serpentine line around a doubt." Can you tell yourself a story or make up a sentence about where or how *your* favorite number or punctuation mark was created? Or where it rose from? Or where the letters of the alphabet lived before they were "snatched up by the mind," like my friend, Prartho, did? (See her poem on the next page.)

You might understand a favorite number, letter, punctuation mark better by writing it on a page and staring at it, imagining what it looks like, what or who it used to be, where it likes to hide, fly, build sand castles . . . maybe even how it moves and what it has to climb to get a better view of the sea or sky. You can also include what your number, letter, punctuation mark isn't, never was, will never be.

FROM *Spell*

Before the alphabet was snatched up
by the mind, it belonged to the body.
Consonants huddled in the crooks of
elbow, ankle and knee, where they thrived
on gossip and potluck dinners,
built cities with jazz clubs and intricate
webs of phone-line and highway.

But the vowels, moon-driven and drunk
on the sound of their own voices,
lived alone in the hollows and caves.

—Prartho Sereno

The Number 7

Seven is a one-winged bird,
graceful as a dream.
Seven is the cane of a blind man,
as old as Egypt. Seven rises
from the ground like a daffodil.
Seven is the shovel the diggers used
to dig up the seven wonders.
Seven is the flag they fly
at the seventh heaven's pearly gate.

—Natalie

Your Turn

The Smaller the Better

Small words are great when your life stories feel too big. Small words dance on your tongue and twirl in your ears, and take up only a hint of white space where they shine on the page. Circle any small word that leaps out at you today. You don't have to know *why* you like a small word. You just do.

Whenever you discover a small word you like, pick it up and toss it in with the rest of your small word collection. How many can you squish onto this list? How big (or small) of a sentence can you build for yourself, using all the small words you've circled today? Share what you write with the wind or a cloud. Stand under a tree. Let your voice grow tall, wide, confident, loud.

fish   hand   time   love

arrow   fire   snore   flag   sand   fight

apple   mile   rocket   snow   song

rain   smoke   dog   wheel

crow   flower   tree   cereal   sliver knife   door   grave   poem   shovel   stone

river   spear   fog   roots   lake

sharp   life   secret   owl   gem   boot

bath   cling   howl   moon   dam   leaf

hole   spark   mist   ash   sky

earth   storm   fern   night   quiet

bear   air   grass   reef   trout

drift   foam   fox   twirl   lace   rush

burn   hour   pale   hill

parade   finger   book   ripple

kiss   hat   sigh   circle   snap

curl   flash   twist   paper   glass

listen   eye   mind   mice   bone

whirl   tiger   cloud   doze   ring   sleep

gust   chant   open   spiral

skull   wax   flap   god   hook   tide

tepee   sauce   grip   roof   claw   brush

A NOTE FROM: *Naomi Shihab Nye*

Dear Writer,

Nothing is too small to notice. The purple martins who live high in their apartment dwelling on a silver pole drop bits of tinsel, green yarn, blue tape when they fly into their holes with twigs and hay for their nests. I find myself picking up their scraps, asking: where did this come from? After a big rain in Texas sometimes, tree frogs which have been hiding— where?—under leaves?—return to the trees and start singing in harmony. Each one of us is packed full of details which might like to glitter for a moment. The world around us is packed full of intriguing, connected details. Writing helps them have a place to shine. Sentences, simple lines, are the ticket. Love your lines and you will have a better time in your life.

Your friend,

Naomi Shihab Nye

A Sample of Naomi Shihab Nye's Writing

FROM *Honeybee*

The Frogs Did Not Forget

> how to do what they do
> > through the huge dry days
> where were they hiding?
> one might lose a tune   abandon a tradition

fall into a crack   but the frogs after the rain
    were singing on six notes
outside the bedroom window's
    tangle of vines
pleasure poking its throaty resonance
    back into   my brain

Naomi Shihab Nye has been writing in a little notebook (green preferred) for a very long time.

The Stanza's Little Room and the Line's Lifeboat

Some kids like to call a stanza "a poetry paragraph." Stanzas of different lengths have different names:

A two-line stanza is called a *couplet*.

A three-line stanza is called a *tercet*.

A four-line stanza is called a *quatrain*.

A five-line stanza is called a *quintain*.

A six-line stanza is called a *sestet*.

A seven-line stanza is called a *heptastich*.

An eight-line stanza is called an *octave*.

In Italian, stanza means "little room of words." You might remember what a stanza is if you can see it as a little room with lines of words inside. You might even pretend you're playing house when you set up your poem. This room (stanza) will have four lines (a quatrain); this room will have three lines (a tercet). And here, at the end, let's put a little two-line room (a couplet). There are an endless number of ways to build your poem's house. Just find the best arrangement that works for you.

You might think of lines that make up the stanzas as a lifeboat. Only so many people can fit in a lifeboat, and only so many words can fit on a line. Lines can be long or short or somewhere in between. Sometimes the longer the line, the more energy and music can build up. Sometimes the shorter the line, the more clipped and halting your words will sound.

But here's the fun part: a sentence does *not* have to end at the end of a line when you're writing a poem. It can. But it can also keep on going and end with that stop-dot in the *middle* of a line. Ditto for commas. Words get to sit on the page in all sorts of ways when you write a poem.

You can tell a poem's a poem even before you read it. Just look for that jagged-ragged right side. Your words can be arranged into a tumbling jumble; they can march straight, cartwheel, even play ring-around-the-rosy. As a poet, you get to put your words into different-length lines and then your lines into different-length stanzas. The next time you write a poem, break it up into different rooms and see how it looks— and reads—on the page. Bottom line, your name comes at the end, so make sure you love the way your poem sounds *and* looks on every page.

Talkin' 'Bout a Tanka

Tanka (Tonka) means "short poem" in Japanese. Tanka are poems made up of 5 lines like this:

line 1 is short

line 2 is long

line 3 is short

line 4 is long

line 5 is long

Tanka use images of real things from your real life that match how you really feel as you're really writing! To do this, a tanka needs strong images: word-pictures you can see, hear, taste, smell, touch. Tanka can be about the shortness of time. Or about love. Or about the seasons. Or even about sadness. They can be about *any* subject your heart needs to write about.

Give yourself some time to feel what you're feeling and then take a tanka for a ride.

Here's a simple way to make a tanka:

Line 1: Name an object from nature (moon, mountain, sun, river, tree, cloud . . .).

Line 2: Choose 3 words that describe your object.

Line 3: What does your object *do*? or *how* does your object move?

Line 4: Where *is* your object in time and space? Be as specific as you can.

Line 5: What do you have that your object doesn't have: no_____, no_____, no_____.

cloud
white, precise, filled with rain
floating above
my mossy-green house
no arms, no voice, no pencil for a poem.

—Katrina

rock
smooth, hard, uniquely shaped
sits and rests
beside a statue
no shirt, no eyes, no feet.

—Evan

Hooked-Together

Have you ever noticed how some words *never* get to sit next to each other? Maybe whoever made the word seating-chart knows they'll start talking, so keeps them apart. But isn't it much more friendly to have a little dash between words . . . so they can at least whisper across the table? How else are they supposed to get to know each other well enough to play on the page? Here's a list for when you want to add silly or surprising relationships to your writing. Play musical chairs and move words around. Make up your own seating chart. Introduce words who are looking for a friend. Come up with your own hooked-together words.

HOOKED-TOGETHER WORDS

firefly-straw	cucumber-tooth	summit-song
broom-rocket	sun-sponge	dawn-blocker
moon-jitters	tender-mover	sweaty-chime
wind-gate	foot-sorrow	cake-whistler
freckle-soup	peacock-pie	hairy-scream
glass-song	knife-bridge	toe-hat
snake-collar	stone-pillow	buzzing-stars
chocolate-meadow	wheel-cry	frog-slipper
leaf-burrow	talking-pouch	summit-jumper

WORDS THAT NEED A FRIEND

ice-	flag-	-mouth
rock-	locket-	-tuba
tentacle-	hoof-	-pocket
doughnut-	mud-	-mummy
mirror-	pancake-	-message

I woke up this morning thinking of funny words. The first was rock-face. Then came chocolate-meadow with ice-mud; pencil-tooth next to cucumber-night, and toe-hat with buzzing-star. Then moon-jitters, foot-whistler, freckle-soup, and hairy-glass. I laughed.

—Katie

Rip the Page!

Cover this page with words you love to whisper, scream, and sing—all those words rip-roaring ready to roll off your tongue and spiral into your ears. Taste them. Especially the strange ones. Yes, even the words you think you *aren't* supposed to say—the shy ones, wacky ones, mean and in-between-ones. Let ANY word be OK to write today. Then smear on some lipstick and plant a *smack-a-roo* or draw a great big heart in the middle of the page. Let this be a valentine for all the words you've come to Earth to love.

Sly Similes and Mighty Metaphors

Similes describe one thing (this page) by comparing it to another thing (a flat cloud), by using *like* or *as*. This page without letters is *like* a flat cloud minus the sky. Writers, especially poets, use similes *all the time* to connect different things (*this* page, *that* cloud), to surprise their imaginations, and to help them see and feel *two* things at once. Similes make your writing and talking voice a lot more fun to listen to, especially when your comparisons come zinging out of your imagination:

My baby sister's fingers are *like* ten worms waiting in line for lunch.

My brother's hair is *as* spiky *as* a cactus when he wakes up.

My cousin's voice is *as* annoying *as* a mosquito buzzing in the dark.

My teeth are *like* a white fence that holds in the pink dog.

Metaphors are another way to compare things. They don't say *this* is like *that*. They say this *is* that. A metaphor lets you move (or transfer) the qualities of one thing to another.

My sister's tongue *is* a long country road, wet and bumpy.

My brother's eyes *are* big blue fish; his nose, a mountain with dark caves holding tiny rocks.

My cousin's ears *are* funnels that catch the wind of every whispered word.

My soul *was* once a grizzly bear and now can take me anywhere.

Can you make up 5 similes (or metaphors) about what different parts of *your* body might look like or wish for? You might write about your imagination and heartbeat, voice and veins, birthmark and breath, lungs and legs, heart and soul . . .

Self-Portrait

My body settles the rain. It wishes to be the sun's brightness.
My arms remind themselves of their friends the elbows.
My knees sway like the hula. My feet feel like marshmallows.
My imagination is like a tornado, as dark as the forest,
as quiet as breath, as fast as a whirlpool, as crazy as rush hour!

—Collin

My Soul

My soul is a kiss in the rain. It's full of surprises and secrets, ready to spill out like a splash from the ocean or a cloud in the desert. My soul is a window of intuition—it's like a hand placed over my heart. It's like a stone that a hammer cannot break. It can be a whirl of delight and a tangle inside a perfect string. My soul is like a mind being fooled or a rush of lightning, running all night. It's the darkness of the past. It's a lonely leaf on an empty tree. My soul is a book that has not yet been read. The hiss, snap, and twist of an angry snake—my soul is words poured on to this page.

—Justice

What's Inside?
You Decide!

Choose one of the 13 lucky containers below. If you can't find one you like, make up another.

Fish Tank   Lunch Box   Shoe   Cereal Bowl   Baseball Cap

Swimming Pool   Magic Trunk   Backpack   Pillowcase

Pocket   Pen Cap   Jewelry Box   Ice Cream Cone

If you could put *anything*—big or small—inside your lucky container, what would it be? What you put inside can even be *bigger* than the container. *Much bigger.* You can include memories, planets, friends, whole cities, entire continents, skyscrapers, monuments, songs, arguments, holidays, feelings, wild (and domestic) animals, eons, and galaxies. . . . The sky is definitely *not* the limit. And, yes, you can even stuff the night sky—complete with a few stars—into your back pocket, if you like.

Sticking out of my green duffel bag is the memory of me falling in front of Gary Ribberal on Mt. Bachelor my first time up on skis; my Uncle Frank's tope is in there, too, along with the pothole from Third Street, 12 baby rattlesnakes, half the Milky Way Galaxy, the Statue of Liberty, and a few million wadded up Band-aids; at the bottom is the tube sock I thought I'd lost and the rope swing from my neighbor's backyard—and, hey, here's the piece of bubblegum I went looking for in the first place. You want half?

Your Turn

A NOTE FROM: *Lemony Snicket*

Dear Young Writer,

Being a writer is like being a mad scientist, because you must work alone, in a lonely room, stitching together something new out of the parts of old things you've found during your secret journeys. For a writer, this means you must spend time eavesdropping on the world, writing down things you see and hear while no one is paying attention to you. This is best done with a notebook, and the first thing you should write down in your notebook is an excuse, so if you are ever caught eavesdropping you will have a good reason why you are standing outside that door, hiding behind that tree, or standing quietly in a room where interesting things are going on, when you have been told to go to bed.

Sincerely,

Lemony Snicket

A Sample of Lemony Snicket's Writing

FROM *The Carnivorous Carnival*

When my workday is over, and I have closed my notebook, hidden my pen, and sawed holes in my rented canoe so that it cannot be found, I often like to spend the evening in conversation with my few surviving friends. Sometimes we discuss literature. Sometimes we discuss the people who are trying to destroy us, and if there is any hope of escaping from them. And sometimes we discuss frightening and troublesome animals that might be nearby. . . .

Lemony Snicket is responsible for a great number of upsetting books, and yet is still at large. There are only two explanations for this situation, and he is currently at work on the third.

Secret-Coded

It's summer vacation. At last. All year, Nick and Collie have been looking forward to hanging out, alone together. But today there's a little brother involved who keeps following the "big guys" around, promising he's going to tell on them for anything they are saying, aren't sharing, did or didn't do. Collie's annoyed. Nick has *had it* with his pipsqueak brother's empty threats. So the two hatch a plan: they'll invent a secret-coded alphabet only *they* can understand. They'll create a secret language all their own that's bound to keep nosy little brothers *and* parents from finding out what they're plotting. Nick snickers. Collie cackles. Then they morph into a tight-lipped team. Meanwhile, the sun is slowly setting. But, who cares? They're on vacation . . . hiding . . . upstairs with paper and pens, a plate of oatmeal cookies, and their inventive imaginations. They can stay up as late as they want, spying and scheming while passing notes in code. What could be better than this?

Your Turn

Use this secret-coded alphabet to write a secret note to your best friend. (Just make sure he can break the code!) Write about a time you and your best friend did something sneaky. Who *didn't* you want to find out? Where were you? If you were going to write a note in code, what would you write? Make up your own code or borrow Nick and Collie's. But be on the lookout for tattletales and pain-in-the-rump 4-year-olds!

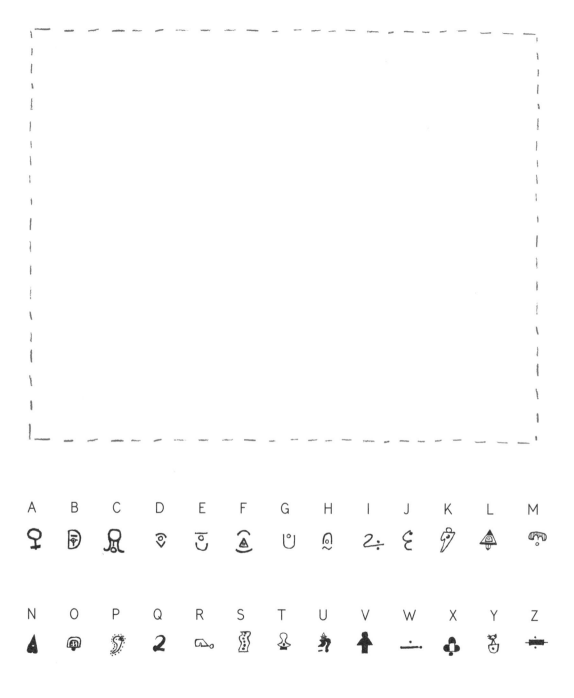

A B C D E F G H I J K L M

N O P Q R S T U V W X Y Z

Alliteration

Listen for alliteration in the following playground tattles and shouts: "Terri, why'd you tell Mr. Thompson I'm too tired to play tag football today?" (Did you hear all those *t* sounds?) Or this one, overheard at recess near the basketball court: "Sam's taking cheap shots and sneaky shoves!" Alliteration is the repetition of similar sounds. Here's a story that uses alliteration with the help of a Snox and a Flax. Listen for all those *"Sssss"* and the *"Lllll"* sounds. What other repeating sounds can you hear? But, wait, what *is* a Snox and a Flax, you ask? Well, I'm not exactly sure. So you decide.

Snox and Flax

The Snox lives near leaves of the past and lets loose a box of seventeen crickets. The Flax lives close to the sound of little thunderclaps and screams, "Stop!" The Snox can fly and loves to collect leaves of lavender-colored luck. The Flax likes to walk along the horizon line and watch each lonely leaf soar into the autumn air then disappear, far and near, after dinner. The Snox and Flax meet in a forest of soft pine where a family of feather-tops suddenly appear late one day, shy and feathery, soft and lost. So the Snox and Flax invite them all to whisper loudly and not to fear, and together they link elbows and walk all night long, singing *la la la la la la la* all the way home.

—Zoe and Karen

To practice alliteration, find your favorite letter today. Then find a few words, real or made-up, to go with your letter. Then just sing some repeated sounds, also known as alliteration, to the page.

HINT: Animals, amphibians, and arachnids *adore* being the acclaimed actors and actresses in any adventure involving alliteration.

The Acrostic's Spine

Do you like hanging upside down? How about twirling in circles? Running as far as your legs—and lungs—can carry you? Well, words do, too. They *love* to hang and twirl; run and spin. If you don't believe me, take a word and tip it on its side. Then stand back as your word becomes an acrostic. . . . For example, take the word "red" and just tip it over, like this:

r
e
d

Some think the word "acrostic" means going a c r o s s the page. But really this word comes from *two* Greek words:

ACRO = "at the end or edge"

STIC = "a line of poetry"

So what *is* this word hanging out at the edge called? *The spine word!*
Why?

Well, it's straight like your spine or the spine (or binding) of this book. The spine word usually comes at the left edge, but you can make a spine word along the right edge, too. Use your spine word to create a new poem, like this:

What I Believe

Red is for
entering
dangerous poems.

The spine word doesn't have to relate to what you write about (though it can). When you play with acrostics, breathe and relax and let your words spill out and dance as fast or slow (long or short) as they need to. Here are some words to get you started.

SPINE WORD SUGGESTIONS

Pancake	Home	Invisible
Ocean	Snake	Death
Mask	Birthday	Recess
Dance	Echo	Curfew
River	Fool	Mother
Road	Breath	Window
Web	Divorce	Voice
Scream	Heart	Sister

WARNING: If you pick a word and still can't write, the spine word has locked you out. It happens. Find another word for your spine. The word that locks you out today might open up tomorrow.

Acrostic Acrobat

Warning: Creating poems with spine words is contagious. You might start out with a plan to write only one, then look up and discover your *entire* page—front and back—is *covered* with acrostics, stretching like Silly Putty across your brain.

Your word can be:

your name

a dog's or cat's name

the word, *acrostic*

any word begging to be tipped

Before reaching for a long word, give a short word a try: *sun* or *flash, thumb* or *luck, song* or *frog* or *fire.* Maybe use one of those small words you circled on pages 29 and 30. The trick to acrostics is NOT to worry if you're doing them right. Forget about right or wrong already. Just hand each worry a mini-suitcase, send them on a little trip, and tip the word you picked.

Your acrostics can be totally serious or not make any sense at all. It's your **choice** because:

Choosing the right word for yourself amidst the

hundreds of thousands of millions

of others is the task, the

inky-tall task of all

creative writers who must not look for anything anywhere

except in the pockets of their own hearts.

Griffin's Luck

Find your
luck in
all that moves
sideways &
horizontal.

Quick Question

Does the sky
over your house ever
open when the
roof is asleep?

Small Fact

Most
animals
rarely
kiss.

Your Turn

Juxtaposition

Take a piece of paper and fold it in half the long way. *Hot-dog style* is how one 10-year-old put it. Just be sure the crease is on the *right*.

Then:

Write down 10 words you like from a word list in this book.

Add a descriptive word in front of each word, if you like.

Flip the paper over (don't unfold it) so the crease is on the *left*.

Then:

Write down the month or season you were born

Write down a day of the week

Write down "the past," "the present," or "the future"

Write down a favorite color (wavering brown)

Write down "My heart"

Write down "My imagination"

Write down a feeling state (joy, sadness, amazement, etc.)

Write down a type of weather (mid-week rain, smooth sunshine)

Write down a small sound (tiny whispers, puppy snores, grunts . . .)

Write down a favorite food

Unfold the paper and write "Poetry Is" at the top (or "My Imagination Is," "Inside My Heart Is," "My Life Is," "Creativity Is" . . .), then combine your lists from either side of the page with the word "of" sitting between each column. Mix and match from each side of the page until you find an example of juxtaposition—putting two unlike things together (side by side) to wake up your ears and make your mouth smile.

Poetry Is

Poetry is a permanent secret locked away in the wings
of a golden parrot. Poetry is a wave washing away seafoam
and quenching the thirst of rain. Poetry is a ghost who died
from smoke and now lives on the sun. Poetry is a creature with
two swords who lies in a history of onions. Poetry is like blue
ice-flying snow and a blazing friendship piercing through
the dusk. Poetry is a federation of cows whose maps all lead
to a lonely egret spiraling back into the shape of mist,
like a pale secret with eyes of flames.

—Colin

A NOTE FROM: *C. M. Mayo*

Dear Creative Writer,

Aren't 4-year-olds pesky? They ask a thousand and eleven questions. Why is the sky blue? Where does the wind go? If potatoes have eyes, can they see the worms in the earth? When Grandpa farted, how come everybody blamed it on Aunt Marty's dachshund? Most 4-year-olds haven't learned to care (very much) what other people think. Some of them even run around without their clothes.

Do you remember being 4? Is your "artist self" young enough to write creatively—or are you just posing for other people? Like a 4-year-old, don't worry too much about what they might think: unzip your heart to the whole world. To the hippo-shaded clouds. The slippery-cold potato peels. Aunt Marty's dachshund, curled up there, tail thumping, under the chair. Have fun, because that's what it's all about.

Sometimes it helps to have a made-up name,

C. M. Mayo

A Sample of C. M. Mayo's Writing

People Who Pat Me (By Picadou)

People who pat me
I sometimes like

But not
The little girl with crumbs on her face
She aimed her fingers at me, she patted me too hard
Her food smells stayed on my head
And not
That man in the blue pants and blue hat
He landed his hand on my head *thunk* like a package
and he moved my fur the wrong way
His shoes stank of sidewalk and hot rubber
"How much did you pay for that dog?" he said to my person
and a lot of other rude nonsense
When he could see we were on our way to the grass!
I like the lady with her hair tucked under an orange scarf
She bent down and I let her hold my chin and stroke my ears
Her hands were gentle like Grandma's
they smelled of mail and cheese sandwich
She had a wavery voice
"Oh," she said, "I wish you were my neighbor!"

C. M. Mayo has been writing since she was a little kid. She lives in Washington, D.C. and Mexico City, and has published a novel, The Last Prince of the Mexican Empire *(Unbridled Books) and many poems, including several which were by her pug dog, Picadou.*

Understanding Everything

Tonight it's just me and the dog. I'm in the kitchen, listening to my favorite song swirl down, like the Frisbee I tossed earlier at the park into a long arc, the dog bounding along, happy. Exhausted now, his panting keeps time with the music as I set out to finish clearing the table and washing the dishes. At the sink, I look out the window at the moon and count the stars, letting my mind drift back, to the exact moment each bright-lit beam began its long journey through time toward my eyes. Rinsing soap bubbles from my hands, I give a nod of thanks to those great flames no longer there. Later, I call a friend to mend a rift that spread between us . . . to apologize for anything insensitive I might have said, but didn't mean. And as the entire night begins to pulse with wind and rain, I replace the phone, change into my pajamas, do a handstand in front of the mirror, and sing out to the dog who has been here all along, look-ing up at me, understanding everything.

Have you ever felt only an animal could understand you? How old were you? Where were you? What was your pet's name? What did you love doing together? What are some things you whispered to him and to no one else? Did she sleep on the floor or up on your bed? Did you feed him your cauliflower and broccoli under the table? What was one of your favorite places to explore together? How did she welcome you home? What did he look like? What was her favorite toy? You might want to read these questions and sit and simply remember. Or you might pick one (or two), find a favorite pen, and with courage as your guide, see where your memories lead . . .

Your Turn

Catch That Cliché

Clichés are pictures made with words that you can see, hear, taste, touch, and feel. A cliché's word-pictures used to be fun and fresh, but got used *so* often they lost *all* their power to wake up your ears and imagination. Clichés are similes that lost their *zing* and now make your writing and speaking voice sound weak and boring. Example: I was busy as a bee planting my winter garden, working my fingers to the bone. By the time the sun set it was as cold as ice and I was as tired as a dog. After reading those last 2 sentences, you're probably yawning (and you should be!). Clichés do that—bore your reader. He looks around for something else to do. Her eyes glaze over. He turns on the radio. She turns up the volume. Your challenge: take an imaginary bow and arrow and shoot down *all* the clichés you find hovering in the air and lurking on the page.

Can you put the *zing* back into these clichés?

Cold as snow   Cold as the edge of_____

Hot as fire   Hot as the front row of a_____

Light as a feather   Light as the inside of_____

Pretty as a picture   Pretty as the sound of_____ (please, no birds!)

Clever as a fox   Clever as the way my dad_____

TIP: The best way to change clichés into treasure is to dig and dig underneath them and not to stop until you've found your own golden language hiding there. Because the genuine 14 karat gold in your words is *always* waiting for your imagination, voice, pencil, and heartbeat to release it.

5 Senses

By playing with combining smell, taste, and touch words with sound and speech words from the lists below, you'll loosen up the kinks and ease the tight spots in your imagination. See how many zany combinations you can create: *A rubbery clap of thunder. A ripe whisper. A rotten scream.* Keep going . . . slip a few into a paragraph you complain is *sooo boring.*

SMELL

sweet	scented	fragrant	perfumed
balmy	spicy	sharp	fresh
earthy	piney	tempting	pungent
rotten	reeking	spoiled	sickly
fishy	musty	moldy	mildewed

TASTE

oily	buttery	salty	bitter
bittersweet	hearty	mellow	sugary
crisp	ripe	bland	sour
fruity	tangy	raw	hot
overripe	burnt	gingery	peppery

TOUCH

cool	slippery	silky	gritty	steamy
spongy	satiny	sandy	rough	velvety
mushy	icy	oily	smooth	sharp
thick	soft	waxy	warm	fleshy
hot	rubbery	furry	dry	dull
thin	elastic	tender	prickly	hairy
fuzzy	feathery	woolly	furry	leathery
crisp	tough	wet	damp	sticky

SOUND

sigh	murmur	whisper	whir	rustle
growl	crash	thud	pitter-patter	thwap
bump	thump	boom	thunder	bang
smash	rasp	clash	jangle	bawl
bark	roar	blare	racket	bleat
clink	mute	still	hush	hubbub

SPEECH

stutter	stammer	giggle	laugh	sing
screech	snort	bellow	chatter	murmur
whisper	whimper	talk	speak	drawl

HINT: Use this white field to explore and store your zaniest smell, taste, touch, sound, speech word-combos.

A gritty, wet sigh murmured up from inside my bath water. But it was only my sister playing one of her ventriloquist tricks. Then came a sharp, bellowing giggle and a moldy hot clink. Help! I yelped.

Suddenly a Story.....

Meeting the President in 5 Words or Less

I met the President. Really. At this party. Standing by the coat closet. He shook my hand. "Karen. Nice to meet you." He shook *my* hand! The President. Well, he wasn't yet. But he would be. And I met him. Can you believe it? I smiled. Then . . . my voice. It caught. You know, how it does. Down around my ankles. I looked at him. Couldn't speak. Not a word. No sound. Not a syllable. No, I did *not* grunt. He waited. Smiled. Kind of concerned. Cute, even. Then moved on. To the woman beside me. She had a voice. "Well, hello there!" He shook her hand. "Carol, nice to meet you." He moved through the room. "Russ, thanks for coming. Sandy, a pleasure." But I was stuck. Right there. In that cramped corner. Wearing a name tag. In such a fancy house. Big vases. Oil paintings. Baby grand piano. People in heels, ties. Trays of tiny sandwiches. Cream cheese, ham. I slid to the floor. I had to . . . crawl. Just to the closet. I reached inside. Found my coat. And my voice. *Don't worry*, it said. *YOU got to shake hands. With the almost-president.* Then I walked home. The long way. With the moon. And my name tag. I couldn't wait. To tell you. Can you believe it? I met the president. Of the entire United States!

Start a story about meeting someone or doing something for the first time. Tell it fast, at a clip, like you're talking to a close friend. That friend who totally *gets* you. That friend you don't have to explain *every little thing* to . . . that friend who doesn't mind when you rush ahead or fast-forward through a thought. In your friend's eyes, you shine. Oh, and just for fun, see if you can tell your story using only 5 words or less per sentence. Afterward, read it and see if you like it. Then go find your friend and read it again.

Your Turn

Rip the Page!

Come up with 1 to 1,000,000 things you're really good at—or wish you were good at. It's OK, be vain. Scribble out your proudest moments and wide-eyed accomplishments—large, medium, small, and super-small—across the page. (I met the president; I can crawl across a room of people and not get stepped on. . . .) Then fold all your well-earned boasting into a paper airplane and let your talents soar.

Onomatopoeia

Onomatopoeia (On-O-Ma-TOE-Pay-A)—say that three times fast. Fine, but what the heck *is* it? It's just a long, 6-syllable word for *sound words*. Words that *make* the *actual sound* or *noise* of what they *mean:*

> Your mom *jiggles* her keys, when she's nervous you're going to be late for school. You *rip* a page from this book and *crumple* it up. It *crackles* as it's *crumpled*. Your Dad's *whistling*, cooking bacon for breakfast. You can hear it *sizzle* in the pan. *Slam* goes the door. *Honk* goes the horn. Oh no, now you really are going to be late! Why can't you just *tip-toe* back to bed with a book to *snuggle* down with and read all day?

Become a collector of sounds. Pick a place you'd like to be right about now: Behind Home Plate. In a Rain Forest. At the Beach. On a Roller Coaster. At an Airport. Boarding a Train. Watching Fireworks. Jumping off a Diving Board. Even Scavenging at the Dump. Ground yourself *anywhere* there's sound. Now, what do you hear at this place you've landed?

You might hear or feel a sound and not know how to spell it. So write: "The sound of a tree growing . . ." or "the sound of a dog dreaming." You can find sound by exploring other senses too: The feel of an unheated swimming pool: *brrrr!* The sound of excitement as your dive breaks the water: *Splash! Yikes! Omygosh* it's *freezing!* The smell of greasy coconut sunscreen being squeezed from a tube: *Yuck!* The taste of a cold slice of watermelon: *Yum!*

At the Dump

Beep! beep! beep!
the garbage truck backs in.
Booooop!
It lowers its tailgate.
Squish, squoosh, splish, sploch.
A Barbie missing an arm,
a strange bright yellow charm,
a broken old record machine,
a banana that is still green.
All of these things fall and fall
and fall
into a pile of trash.
Vroom!
The truck starts up the hill.
Crash!
The truck flips over backwards
and starts down the hill.
Bam! Flip. Bam! Flip. Squish!
In . . .
to . . .
the . . .
trash!

—Jack

Action-Packed!

Let's say you're in the middle of writing an adventure story. Your brainy hero's hanging off a cliff, holding on to the last brittle branch of some scrawny tree . . . then, *SNAP!* In the distance, the bad guys are about to *ZOOM* away. But wait, isn't that your hero *dashing* up behind them? He survived the fall. He didn't go *SPLAT,* after all. *Hip, hip hooray!* yells the entire town. Your hero, blushing, *Aw shucks,* waves to his fans. When you need your words to imitate the sound, noise, action of *what* your words mean, just look at this list to add a flash-dash of *pizzazz.*

Whooo-sh	Yippy	OOZE
HISS	THUMP	SPLAT
Jeeez!	SHA-ZAM	Thwack
BUZZ	eeek!	Boing
Ripple	Plop	Buuuuurrpp!
Crunch	yippity	gurgling
Weeeee!	Aaaahhh!	rustle
Lickety-split	thing-a-ma-jig	blah blah blah
gooey	slurp	ribbit
ZING	SNAP	slither

BASH	BAROOOM	Munch
POP	rat-a-tat-tat	CRASH
Vroom	click	WHEW
Sizzle	crackle	Pooof
Mmmmmm	hoot	Zing
splash	YUM!	thud

When you need a word to make the sound of what it does but aren't having any luck finding the word you need, that's the time to make one up.

Dear Writer:

If you're about to sit down and craft an action-adventure story of your own, then remember the single most important ingredient: tension. Tension is what will propel your story forward and compel your reader to keep flipping the page. Think of a singular rubber band. If you pull the two ends, it lengthens and tightens. There's tension on it. Now, keep pulling it until, under pressure, the band explodes into two pieces with a sharp *snap*! That's exactly the feeling you want to create for your reader as the story moves and nears its end. Your main character needs to be placed in one dire situation after another (with only brief periods of relief) until the reader feels so emotionally on edge that he or she nearly *snaps* with anxiety! Then, when the tension has broken, resolve things for your character (and your reader) in a comforting way. Doing so will make sure that your reader is not only satisfied with the ending, but pleased that he or she decided to take this journey with you.

Sincerely,
Elizabeth

A Sample of Elizabeth Singer Hunt's Writing

FROM *Secret Agent Jack Stalwart:*
The Escape of the Deadly Dinosaur

Slowly, an enormous green head lowered itself through what used to be the doorway, and into the hallway. It was so massive that it barely fit through the door frame. Its eyes, which were black and bulging, were roaming up and down the hall. The hundreds of teeth that lined its wide jaws were tall, thin, and razor-sharp. ... *ROAR!* Its fearsome roar made Jack jump. Although he hadn't seen its body yet, Jack recognized the head from Lewis Porter's book. It was the head of the most ferocious carnivore of the late Jurassic. It was the Allosaurus. And Thomas had brought it to life in his very own bedroom.

Elizabeth Singer Hunt is the author of the popular Secret Agent Jack Stalwart series for younger readers. Never having studied writing before, Elizabeth began penning her first Jack Stalwart story in 2002. She lives in Northern California with her husband and two children.

Nothing, You Got That?

I watch as the blue-hooded boy in the back row introduces himself to the substitute as *Just Matt*. I try not to stare but notice he just sits there, his face hard, pieces of dried grass clinging to a dirty pant leg. He draws dark circles across the bottom half of the lined paper in front of him and calls it *The Nothing*. He says there isn't anything inside his imagination today: no dogs, no trees, not even the storm that passed through his backyard the night before, tipping over the trash bins his mom put out too early in the week; the ones his dad yelled at her for while Matt stayed upstairs with his brother. Turns out, this morning his mom yelled at him. He was going to be late for school again and if she told him once, she told him a hundred times: she didn't have time for this today. She didn't want to hear another word out of him. *Nothing. You got that?*

What *aren't* you going to write about? What gets you angry, annoyed, frustrated, sad, yelling-mad? Spit out everything you don't want to say. Everything you refuse. All that you despise. You might start every sentence with: I'M NOT GOING TO WRITE ABOUT . . . then go on to groan, gripe, complain about everything you refuse to talk about. Be as rude, loud, and lonely as you dare. The page won't care. It knows how to just sit there and listen.

Your Turn

Questions Without Answers

One of the last books Chilean poet Pablo Neruda wrote was *The Book of Questions,* where he asked 74 unanswerable questions in the form of *short poems.* But Pablo Neruda wasn't asking these poem-questions to find out information, or to have someone raise their hand and give him the right answer. The questions he asked were posed simply because they engaged, expanded, and amused his imagination. Have you ever asked a question for the sheer pleasure of asking it, a question that you didn't want or need to have answered? To ask a question this way can feel sort of strange at first. Your imagination might need a little time to catch up to this new way of thinking. It helps to remind yourself that these questions *don't have to be true*. It also helps to give your imagination a long leash to wander, to sniff behind things and to make strange connections. Just remember, you don't have to *get* anywhere. You *never* have to arrive at a town called *Answer*.

If iced-over stones are only in my dreams,
then what is the silent lightning for?

—Claire

Why do cowboys always die two miles out?
Is the raccoon masked because someone's after him too?

—Nick

What does the creek of my life think
about the crow-red wind?

—Kailey

Do scrambled-up memories fall into extinct volcanoes?
I hear their whispers echoing, but what are they saying?

—Kendall

What puts people in a twilight mood—
the humble past or the dark future?

—Samuel

Why don't autumn leaves stay in their pajamas?
Why doesn't winter take off its raincoat and join spring?

—Hayley

Do pen caps hold the key to literature or is it the drip of
pasta sauce smudged on the lonely corner of the page?

—Salem

Your Turn

What do you *wonder* about? Start your wondering lines with one of these words: *Who, What, Where, Why, How, When, Could, Do, Is, It, If, Would, Could . . .*

Change Your Point of View

Each time you tell a story or recount something that happened, like that time your sister burst into you room without knocking and you called for your mom, you're telling what happened from *your* Point of View (POV). Literally the position from which you watched that room-burst happen. What you saw (the door swing wide) and what you heard (your sister scream your name). Basically the events of the story experienced through your (or your main character's) eyes and ears, heart and feelings.

First Person POV uses "I" to tell the story. *I was just sitting there on my bed reading* A Wrinkle in Time *and she swung my door wide without knocking and screamed at me!* Your sister's First Person account of the story might go like this, *I opened the door and said her name, because I couldn't wait to share my pack of Milk Duds.* In story writing, First Person POV uses "I" to tell the story.

Second Person POV uses "You" to tell the story. *You were just sitting on your bed reading, when your sister burst into your room!* Or *You burst into the room and yelled your sister's name, excited to share your box of Milk Duds.* Sometimes you might choose this Second Person POV to achieve a little distance for yourself.

Third Person POV uses "He" and "She" to tell the story. *She was sitting on her bed thinking about starting her homework, and her sister burst into the room and started yelling, waving a box of Milk Duds in her face like the big tease that she is.* This POV can give you a little mask or veil from which to tell your story.

You probably write (and talk) from First Person POV a lot. Sometimes it's fun to write—and even talk—from Second or Third Person POV. It gives you some distance and objectivity for you to view *your* life. Plus it's fun to talk about and refer to things you did or will do as if you were talking about someone else.

If you want to literally practice writing from a different point of view, just change the spot from which you write: Twirl in a circle until you're dizzy then write what you see and how you see it, using Second Person POV . . . *You are falling sideways through the spinning world, seeing everything at a slant* . . . (then name a few of these everythings).

Sit under the kitchen table and write about feet, small animals, and dust bunnies, using Third Person POV: *She (or he) sat under the kitchen table, counting each person's shoes. Her mom's black heels meant she'd be leaving soon for work; her dad's brown slippers meant he was staying home with a cold; her sister's tap shoes meant she'd soon be dancing . . .*

Other ideas to help you play with POV:

Hide in the corner and write as a spy.

Imagine yourself up in an airplane, looking down on your life, and write as an all-knowing wizard.

Think of your favorite villain and write from his/her POV.

Your way isn't anyone else's way. Play with the pronouns: I, We, You, He, She.

Sunday Morning (from Scout's POV)

Mom's taking a shower; Dad's still in bed. I scratch their door—
they pretend not to hear. Outside, I squeeze through the gap in the
fence that I overheard Mom tell the neighbor: "Oh, Scout can't fit
through that." The morning I don't get my kibble on time (I like it
by 9 a.m.) I decide to show them who's boss. I walk the road that
winds to the creek where I sniff, romp, and roam. But when I try to
find my way home, the streets all look the same. I don't know that
Mom has gone searching for me, posting flyers with the photo from
Christmas—*LOST DOG*. Dad has phoned the Sheriff, who wan-
dered our backyard. A man in a red cap whistles, "Here, puppy!"
Then bends to read my collar. We take a fast ride in his Jeep, over
a steep hill. And . . . *Dad!* I gaze up when he opens the front door.
He takes my face in his hands, thanks the nice man, and sends me
off down the hall. Mom cries when she learns of my return. She
kisses me and shows me the sign: LOST DOG. Over my bed, she
tapes it to the wall and pours a cup of kibble into my bowl—which
is what I'd said I had wanted, all along. So it has worked, you see.
I now get my breakfast on time.

Let The Moon Speak

Anything can speak in a poem. Choose something non-human, like the moon, a raccoon, the night, a flashlight, running water, a tree, a feather, even fire. . . . Then let each thing speak *through* you. The things you choose to let speak don't have to be related to each other. Though they can, if you like. You can even let one thing speak *about* or *to* the other things, the way my poet-pal, Grace Marie Grafton, does in her poem below.

What Speaks

Moon says,
I don't know what to do
about this shadow that
keeps crawling on me.

Raccoon says,
Moon just makes it
harder for me—
Give me the moonless night.

Night says,
I don't mean anything by it.

I just keep losing
that blasted flashlight.

Flashlight says,
I wish I were water.
This fire in my gut
makes me want to die.

Water says,
Slum, sluum,
Slumum, wurgle, whirl,
Slluuupp. . . . Here
I'm going to rest awhile.

—Grace Marie Grafton

Your Turn

What will you let speak?

What does tree say?

— — — — — — — — — — — — — — — — — —

Does flame have a voice?

— — — — — — — — — — — — — — — — — —

What does fire wish for?

— — — — — — — — — — — — — — — — — —

What talks back to the harmless moon?

— — — — — — — — — — — — — — — — — —

Voice

If you're a singer—or a poet or a storyteller—your voice is your most valuable instrument. And just as you wouldn't pick up your violin or guitar without tuning it first, it's important to clear your throat and sing a few *do, re, mi, fa, so, la, tee dos* before you read a story or recite a poem.

Your voice can also be heard on the page, through the words you choose *and* the way you choose to arrange them. If you're sad or scared, maybe you'll write in a whisper. If you're feeling left out or ignored, maybe you'll write in a scream. Just as you have a unique set of fingerprints and taste buds, you also have a unique way of sounding to the world—both *in* the air and *on* the page: careful, happy, confident, gentle, nervous, controlling, humorous, knee-slapping.

To hear two distinct voices, record a conversation with your cat—or someone or something very different from you. Of course, you'll be writing both sides of the conversation, but you'll need to use two different voices. Put whatever is spoken into "quotes"—this is called dialogue. Write as you would *talk* out loud to any real or made-up creature. Here's how my cat— given his unique set of claws and personality—might talk, if English were his first language. Turns out, my small gray and white tabby has a *big* attitude, face-to-face *and* on the page.

Me: "Here, Clive!"

C: "You actually think I'm going to come when called?"

Me: "Did someone get up on the wrong side of his kitty bed this morning?

C: "Hello, I'm nocturnal. I was hunting. All night, if you must know. There are no more mice in America, not that it's any of your business. Though I do plan to sleep on every bed in the house today, thank you very much. And for your information, no one calls it *a kitty bed.*"

Me: "Some milk, maybe?"

C: "Add tuna fish tid-bits to that order, arrange it on a clean plate, and I'll consider it."

Me: "Come on, Clive. Where's my sweet guy?"

C: "You're doing it again, calling me."

Me: "You know, Clive, the dog is never rude."

C: "Hello. Earth to Karen: the dog had his brain removed."

Dear Young Poet,

One of the things that "famous" writers recognize is that every single person on the face of the earth is different: each person sees the world in a different way, smells things differently, likes some foods and not other foods, likes some music and not others. You are *you*. There has never been a *you* like *you* before. Write *you*. Let the world see *you*. Let the world see the world the way *you* see the world, and you'll never run into the idea that you don't have anything new or interesting to say. So the best thing to do is look around you, but don't just look: touch the stone wall, smell the flowers, taste your grandmother's Sunday dinner, listen to a new kind of music—or traffic sounds—and then write. It's your voice. Use it.

All the best,
Moira

A Sample of Moira Egan's Writing

Hearts & Stones

I have a friend who collects heart-shaped stones.
She plucks them out of nowhere, catching glints
and glimmers of this gift, the earth present-
ing chthonic valentines to her alone.
Of marble, crystal, sandstone, fossil, quartz—

her vast collection spans a glacier's age.
It's said collectors are trying to assuage
a hole within, some awful primal loss.
If that's the case, I want to tell her that
we all have empty spaces, awful scars.
Even the earth accretes itself in layers;
that force creates both precious stones and granite.
And if her heart-shaped stones reflect the one inside,
I want to tell her every heart is petrified.

Moira Egan is a poet who lives in Italy, a discus throw from the Coliseum in Rome. She has a 12-year-old cat named Iris, and works with her husband translating poetry from English to Italian. Her first book, Cleave, *was nominated for the National Book Award.*

Go Inside a Stone

Before you read any further, set this book down, go outside, and find a stone. Once you've found the right one for you, sit down and look it over. Let the stone you've chosen come alive inside the palm of your hand. Bend in close and listen. Smell it. (Maybe even lick it.) Your stone might be gray and white and remind you of that spotted dog who followed you home. Or it might be the shape of the Earth, spinning. Or a spaceship, rescuing a planet on fire. Some stones are brave. Some are shy. Some have the power to look you in the eye. Some help the universe of your imagination expand until you're deep inside your own jagged, smooth, lopsided rocky wildness of stone-ness. You might decide to stop right here. But, if you want to venture *inside,* buckle your seatbelt. Inside your stone, you might find boot prints in the snow, a flock of sparrows, a lost memory returning, or a never-ending bend in time. Charles Simic wrote a poem titled "Stone" and discovered, "From the outside the stone is a riddle: / No one knows how to answer it." His poem ends with an image of what might be found on the inside of a stone. What will *you* discover inside your special stone? How will *your* stone poem end?

Even though no two stones are exactly alike, just as no two poets are exactly alike, you can still use the same title "Stone" for your poem.

Stone

I would like to go into a stone.
Not to be taken, but to rest.
My smooth sides make friends with others.
No matter where I go, time flies by and by and away.
Things rub side to side, but I don't mind.
My colors are from the outside.
Things come and go, but I stay right here.
My beautiful sound goes with the flow of the afternoon river.
I travel the world by hand—
And the world is my great home.

—Cody

Your Turn

Rip the Page!

A famous writer named Joseph Conrad said, "Give me the right word . . . and I will move the world." Find a letter you like, crack open a dictionary, and move your world by finding words you haven't used in a while (or ever!). Interview a friend about their favorite letter and matching words. (Today I picked *P* because I'm pooped from piling cairns—they're stacked on the next page—then I sat with the dictionary propped on a pillow and found some more words I didn't know I liked: *pterodactyl, pronghorn, pogo stick, ping-pong, polliwog, piccolo, passport, pen knife, Patagonia . . .*) When you're ready, turn this page into something that starts with your letter. I folded my page into the smallest puck I could crease for a game of indoor hockey.

Try This....

W⊙rd Cairns

Since humans first roamed the planet, *cairns*—rocks from mountainsides stacked into piles and shapes—have helped fellow travelers mark their journey by pointing the way in the right direction. Pick a letter—maybe the one from the last page—and gather up words that start with this letter. Write them one on top of the other. An apricot can hold up Antarctica. A piece of lint is strong enough to balance a Lamborghini. Put your mom at the base of Mt. Everest. Make different-shaped cairns to point the way on to the next page. Or keep adding words to the ones below. They don't have to stack up straight and balance exactly. Toss more around the base. Build up the sides. Jumble them into teetering towers that almost fall but don't. Using words from one of your cairns, write a story or poem about a time you got lost and then found your way home.

LAMBORGHINI	Mt. Everest	Antarctica
Leaf-shadows	*Mitten*	Army ants
Loneliness	Mouse	**ASTEROIDS**
Ladybug	MANGO	Auditorium
LIONESS	Mongoose	ARITHMETIC
Lint	Messy *room*	**Alligator**
	Mom	Anxiety
		Apricot

Your Turn

A Wave of Silence

Before diving into silence, make time for some noise. Warn your parents, though, that your noise-making's for a soon-to-be quiet creative writing experiment, so they don't wonder, *hey, what's going on in there?!* Noise-making ideas include: slamming doors and drawers (watch those fingers!), stomping, clapping, whistling, chanting, pounding, banging, shrieking, moaning, wheezing, laughing, screaming, snorting, sneezing, and even re-creating a tantrum from when you were three. For advanced noise-makers: perform all of the above at the same time.

After making as much noise as your head, heart, ears, and parents can stand, pick up a pen. Don't wait. Don't hesitate. Let the wave of silence crash through you. Follow your heartbeat. It might feel strange—and scary—at first, but risk diving into *everything* you're feeling and still hearing. Even fear. (Especially fear.) Sometimes whatever you *don't* want to write about is where your best material for writing lives. So wade into the hushed unknown. Ride your own personal wave of silence. Splash the undertow of your answers—and echoes—across the tide of the page.

What Silence Is Like

Stars gleaming in the night. Deserted hills. Boats drifting in the distance. A dim light. Fire dancing. Shadows of forgotten people. Not fireworks at night. Not a football game. Not a crackle of lightning. But fog creeping over the hill. An Indian hunting in the woods. A school of fish. Candles flickering inside pumpkins.

—Aidan

What Silence Was Like

It was like mother nature, calling me.
It said it like nobody was there.
Silence looked like everybody had disappeared.
It was like I was just there, all alone.
I heard the trees calling *Janelle, Janelle* . . .
In a safe way, I heard birds inside of me.
The birds chirped, *I love you.*

—Janelle

Your Turn

98

Far Out

The symbol for infinity looks like an 8 resting on its side. And since infinity never ends, it's pretty much as far out there as you can get. Some say space never ends . . . that it keeps e x p a n d i n g *forever.* How far *out there* can you imagine going? What might you pass through to get there? *(I pass 7 flying saucers on my way through a light-year of quasars and constellations of shooting stars . . . getting to infinity could take a while, so I unwrap a Luna Bar . . .)*

Draw a series of horizontal and vertical lines to form a matrix and arrange the 56 words below (and any other words you might need) into a short story to take you on your journey. Or use these words for a poem about feeling safe at home and stay right here on Earth.

starlight	particles	universe	meteorite
reflection	fragments	fuzzy	constellations
nova	streak	North Star	shooting
rotate	absorb	ether	black hole
collapse	light years	concentric	supernova
orbit	spiral	cluster	burst
flying saucer	earthshine	speed	asteroid
hydrogen	glow	halo	patterns

gravity	Milky Way	quasar	eclipse
cluster	nebula	zenith	galaxy
Big Dipper	doppelgänger	Orion	Little Dipper
Red Giant	atom	giant	dust
rings	explosive	pulsing	moons
electron	intelligence	satellite	particle
solar flares	radiant	comet	airglow
brightness	shadow	planetary	shower

With an explosion at sunrise, my blast-off begins; my solar-powered craft a streak of blazing heat. From my window, I watch Earth recede into a memory of being held as a baby. I shoot past stars and spinning planets of gas and ice, glowing like over-sized fireflies. My mind, a halo of rotating spirals as I seek out new forms of intelligent life. With my body suctioned deep into my seat, my imagination accelerates to warp-speed. I've just disappeared into the future where there's no time left to be sad or to wave good-bye to the cosmic safety known as the Milky Way.

Nouns and Verbs Are Your Friends

A noun's a part of speech that names a person, place, or thing. You know, something you can reach out and actually *touch*.

A verb is a word that shows action. A verb *describes* what a noun does.

The **boy** *walks* into the **room**.

Boy and **room** are both nouns. We can touch the boy. We can touch the room. How does the boy get into the room? He **walks.** Walks is the action; it's what the boy does. Walk is the *verb* . . .

. . . *Boring!*

What are some *other ways* this boy might get into that room? By finding the right verb, your reader will learn *a lot* about this kid, without you having to utter a word. Spending time choosing the right verb is a good way to avoid using adverbs—which describe verbs (the boy walked *quickly*). Adverbs can be like false friends, if used too often, so stick with the true-blue heartbeat of any sentence—the verb. Verbs are what carry the *feeling* of this boy's thoughts and ideas.

Exciting Verbs

There are so many more interesting ways for this boy to enter that room besides simply walking through the doorway. Take a look at the list below. Fill in the blanks using one or two (or more) of the verbs offered (or use some of your own). Then, circle some verbs in your stories and poems and experiment with giving them "verb vitamins." See what exciting new verbs they change into. Also, consider writing a few lines about how the nameless boy *leaves* the room, and where he runs next . . . while continuing to use vivid verbs.

The boy_____and _____ into the room.

cartwheels	ping-pongs	rushes
careens	trudges	break-dances
tumbles	squeezes	coughs
jumps	slides	hulas
hopscotches	bolts	bicycles
skips	slumps	tip-toes
flies	moonwalks	back-flips
somersaults	creeps	tunnels
twists	spins	pole vaults
crawls	jack-knifes	rolls
parachutes	swung	climbs (a window's open!)

Dear Friend:

I don't know of any poet who, in the beginning of his or her art, has not carried around a book of poems. For me, in the early seventies, I swung in my mitts W. S. Merwin's *The Carrier of Ladders* and Charles Simic's *Dismantling the Silence*, two books that fed my curiosity about the world inside their creative minds. I was born and raised in Fresno, California, and the poetic landscape of each of these titles was different from the world around me. I welcomed this landscape, and welcomed them. I then discovered an even weightier world in the shape of Pablo Neruda, master of them all. I learned from others by intense reading that began with the natural light of morning and ended at night when I snapped off the bedroom lamp.

Stay strong,

Gary Soto

A Sample of Gary Soto's Writing

Looking Around, Believing

How strange that we can begin at any time.
With two feet we get down the street.
With a hand we undo the rose.
With an eye we lift up the peach tree

And hold it up to the wind—white blossoms
At our feet. Like today. I started
In the yard with my daughter,
With my wife poking at a potted geranium,
And now I am walking down the street,
Amazed that the sun is only so high,
Just over the roof, and a child
Is singing through a rolled newspaper
And a terrier is leaping like a flea
And at the bakery I pass, a palm,
Like a suctioning starfish, is pressed
To the window. We're keeping busy —
This way, that way, we're making shadows
Where sunlight was, making words
Where there was only noise in the trees.

Gary Soto is author of more than thirty books, including Baseball in April, Taking Sides, Buried Onions, The Afterlife, Neighborhood Odes, *and* New and Selected Poems. *The Gary Soto Literary Museum opens at Fresno City College in fall 2010.*

Did You Hear That?

In the middle of the night, the walls and floors of my house stretch in their sleep, the skylight at the end of the hall snores, and the small square window that leaks in moonlight sighs. At the bottom of the stairs, there's a series of clicks and shivers while the sound the dark makes is like a groan curled up on its side. My cat and dog hear it. So do the sheep, grazing through my dreams. There are millions of tiny, teetering, leaning sounds our human hearing can't quite reach. It's hard to explain, but each room, season, school, planet, rock, bone, twig, pencil, cell, each . . . *everything* carries its own "sound-feeling." Sometimes when I sit on the ground near my garden, close my eyes, and listen with my imagination turned on high and spread out wide, I can catch a few of these "invisible" sound-feelings. But only if I can get quiet enough on the inside, and fine tune the ears of my heart. Only then can I hear the sounds of wasps being born, tree branches reaching, stars burning, *and* all those meteors crashing on the dark side of the moon.

Sometimes sound—the sounds you hear *and* the sounds you think you can't hear—is all you really need to tell a story or to write a poem. The dare-to-believe-in-yourself soccer sounds, Monopoly sounds, jumbled-up *please-don't-forget-me* sounds, underground-lost-in-the-soul-of-winter sounds. Even (and especially) the sounds that live *within* other sounds (the thrum of fear, the patience of tree roots). Listen all day. Stay up all night. Capture them all, each echo of every sound you care enough to pay attention to. Record the next five sounds that insist upon your writing them down.

Your Turn

Rip the Page!

Make a tally of things that thrill you *and* things that disappoint you. Then find your most excellent exclamations to go with each. You know, lightning storms: YOW-ZA! Slumber party: YIPPEE! Our team lost by 1 point: JEEZ! Brussels sprouts: OMYGOSH! See how many exclamation—and exclamation points—can be paired with each thrilling or troubling thing. Attach one of your shouts to a chopstick, and wave it high the next time something makes you laugh or cry.

Baseball Lingo

You probably have a few friends like Jim, Ellen, Boots, and Pierre—who *love* baseball. OK, so maybe Jim's a bit more crazy about the sport than the others, but they've all been to the Hall of Fame in Cooperstown, New York. They all know the stats of their favorite players (mostly from the Boston Red Sox). They're all fluent in "Baseball Lingo."

all-star	Fenway	knuckleball	earned run average
inning	triple A	bean ball	slider
wild pitch	strike out	pop fly	base hit
frozen rope	blooper	Texas Leaguer	screaming line drive
double play	stolen bases	strike zone	dugout
Green Monster	Peskey's pole	mound	curveball
batting average	bunt	suicide squeeze	fastball
high cheese	stealing home	major league	caught in a pickle
hot corner	triple	double	put out
line drive	error	grand slam	change-up
splitter	sacrifice	seeing-eye single	box score
stolen bases	base on balls	World Series	shortstop

If baseball's not the sport you long for—dream about, want to be playing, watching, talking about *all the time*—then what is? Nothing's stopping you from making your own word-lingo list. Maybe you'll write a mini description for your favorite sport lingo words for someone who has no clue what they mean and would enjoy hanging out with you and watching (playing, even) if they knew the rules.

A List of Lists

You can make a poem from a list of just about anything: *15 Things That Make Me Happy. 10 Things I Thought About As I Walked Home From School Today. All the Places My Cat Prowls. Who Gets What When I Die. 3 Secrets. Every Place I've Ever Slept. 27 Things I Can't Hear With Human Ears. How to be a Great Baseball Player. What My Father Taught Me.* Even the *title* of your list-poem can be a list: *My Favorite Teacher, Dessert, Hiding Place, Person, Color, Number, Road Sign, Smell, Cussword, Song, Season, and Sport.* On and on, the list of lists unravels. Every time you find a new subject for a list-poem, come back to this page and add it to your list of list-poem ideas. When you're finally ready to write, pick a title and let out a sigh.

How to be a Great Baseball Player

Be a good sport.
Say "hi" to the umpire.
If you strike out, say to yourself, *I'll try again next time.*
Try to hit balls.
Be happy if you hit a homerun.
When you're fielding, don't swear too much.
Ditto if someone hits a double, or a triple . . .
If you win a world series, celebrate for 12 hours.
If you lose, say, "We'll win next year."

—Quirae

14 Things That Make Me Happy

Finding wasp nests in the backyard with my cousin
Not loading the dishwasher after dinner
Mice
When my mom says, *good night, sleep tight*
Sitting in front of a fire
When my dad gets home from work
Piano lessons being canceled
My birthday
My sister's smile
Rainstorms
The smell of lavender
Saturday morning
Fudge without nuts
My dog's face in the window

—Group poem

Your Turn

Spoonerisms

Spoonerisms are sooooo fun. They're a type of pun—a play on words—where, when you're speaking, you accidentally switch the letters or sounds of two words—and make someone laugh. They're named after William Spooner, a teacher, who made *lots* of errors when he spoke. One day, he accused a student of missing his history lecture but accidentally said: "You hissed my mystery lecture!" When he meant to say, "You have wasted a whole term!" It came out, "You have tasted a whole worm!" Thanks to William, Spoonerisms were born. Now you get to play with words this way, too. Swap a few consonants and vowels around and play with creating some silly spoonerism sentences. Reverse letters and syllables, and see what comes off the tip of your tongue. Maybe create a character based on William Spooner who, every time he opens his mouth, talks this way, too.

William meant to say the following, but guess how it came out instead?

A *crushing blow* became:

— — — — — — — — — — — — — — — — — — — —

You were *lighting* a *fire* in the quad became:

— — — — — — — — — — — — — — — — — — —

Is the *dean busy?* became:

— — — — — — — — — — — — — — — — — — —

The last book by Shel Silverstein is titled *Runny Babbit: A Billy Sook*. This is the best example of spoonerisms yet. Check it out of the library. It's a guaranteed laugh.

My Rittle Leminders for Wreative Criters

TOLLOW THE FRAIL   TAKE MIME LO TAUGH

MELIEVE IN BAGIC!   LAY ATTENTION TO YOUR PIFE

RAKE TISKS   WOOL AROUND WITH FORDS

YURPRISE SOURSELF!   CEAVE LOOKIES FOR MOUR YUSE

Try This....

A Real-Life Hero

Who's one of your real-life heroes? Pick 3 traits to go with this person. Maybe he has the kindest eyes or the biggest feet or rides the fastest 3-wheeled bicycle. Maybe her voice reminds you of rain. Maybe he gets angry when someone mispronounces his name. Sit a while and think about something you'd like to ask or tell this person. (Your hero can even be a person who is no longer living.)

Now write your real-life hero a note as though you were actually having a little chat or conversation with them. Start your note with the line: "I remember when you_____" (you fill in the blank). You can use "I remember . . ." as often as you like, but since notes are meant to be short, you don't have to go on and on. Just say or ask the truest thing in your heart today. Oh, and you might want to pay attention to the last word you put on each line; the last word of a line is the place to put strong words. You know, words you can see or reach out and touch, like *face, plane, homeless, jelly rolls, birthday, fuzzy green, teeth,* etc. OK, so who will you write—or pass—your note to?

Note to Roberto Clemente

I remember when you stepped up
to bat for the first time
and they mispronounced your last name.
If I could have seen the anger in your face,
I would have known how it feels.
I remember when you got your 3,000th hit.
I remember when you flew on the plane
to send help to the homeless.
I remember when you died in that plane crash.
Whenever I step up to bat, I remember you.

—Irvin

Dear Grandpa Alex

I remember when you babysat
and brought me jelly rolls
from your bakery in Manhattan.
You brought me books and a smile,
and wore a short-sleeve shirt
with brown pants pulled up high,
looking like a Grandpa should.
I remember when you visited us in California,
and how you brought me a ring
for my eighth birthday,
the last gift Grandma picked out:
heart-shaped and fuzzy green, my birthstone.
I remember how we sat out back
on lawn chairs and you lectured me
on teeth and the importance of dentists.
I liked how you had all your own teeth,
unlike other grandpas

who kept theirs floating in a jar.
I remember when I cried,
wishing you were still near
with your books and your smile,
eating jelly rolls with Grandma
and looking like a grandpa should.
P.S. I wear the ring on a chain
near my heart and still have
all my own teeth.

—Cathy Carmedelle

Your Turn

A NOTE FROM: *Lucille Clifton*

Dear Young Writer,

Ignore the answers, follow the questions, they will take you where you need to go.

Love, *Lucille*

A Sample of Lucille Clifton's Writing

note, passed to superman

sweet jesus, superman,
if i had seen you
dressed in your blue suit
i would have known you.
maybe that choirboy clark
can stand around
listening to stories
but not you, not with
metropolis to save
and every crook in town
filthy with kryptonite.
lord, man of steel,
i understand the cape,
the leggings, the whole
ball of wax.
you can trust me,
there is no planet stranger
than the one I'm from.

Lucille Clifton received a National Book Award in 2000 for Blessing the Boats. *She was the author of over 20 children's books that centered on the African-American experience.*

Rip the Page!

There's a Japanese belief where the gods will grant a sick person's wish to be well again if the person makes a thousand cranes. Write the name of someone you know who might be sad or sick or in need of some special cheering up in 999 different ways all over this page (backward; upside down; right to left; in Japanese; while holding a pen between your teeth . . .). Then crease their name into a paper crane and hang it by your bed. Every time you look at it, send out long, light-filled thought-rays of health and happiness to this person that you love.

Memories Never Die

I stop at Rachel's desk and she tells me that she doesn't like writing about herself.

"I'm better at remembering my dad," she says. "He died."

I tell her she can write about anyone and this is what she writes.

My Dad

I'm thankful I got to spend all those wonderful 7 years bike riding across Yosemite Valley with my dad, and going to the beach when it was foggy and to the pool on a hot muggy day. I remember how we hiked up to a man-made pond and saw lots of fish, including our favorite, the rainbow one with gold on its tips.

She writes straight through until recess.

My dad is like a secret that I could never keep; his happiness like a cheetah running with his cubs into the horizon; his trust like a hawk swooping for its prey.

When it's time for me to go, she gives me permission to take her paper home. Later, I sit at my desk and finish reading what she was brave enough to share with the page:

Now when I go to Yosemite, the world stops shining, the moon stops coming up, the crickets stop chirping, and God stops making it rain. The horses stop galloping and the fish stop swimming and the moon stops talking to the sun. I wish my dad could be here, but for all I know he's hiking Mt. Everest right now with a friend.

—Rachel

Think of someone special who you love and feel super-close to. This person can be alive, or might no longer be living. All that matters is the feeling you hold inside your heart about this person. Because that feeling *never* dies. You might think of something they gave you, like a locket or a shell, or something they taught you to do, like knit a scarf or do a back-flip. You might recount a story they liked to tell (and retell), a special place you traveled together, or where you imagine they are right now. Who—and what—are you good at remembering?

Your Turn

Before I Wrote This

Memory is a powerful tool. Like most kids, you probably have a steel-trap memory and can remember what your teacher said or promised, and what your parents did or didn't do *down to the last detail* of date, dialogue, disagreement, and description. Here's a challenge: write down everything you did, in the order in which you did it, *before* you picked up your pen or pencil to write today. A team of Dutch scientists were able to prove that walking backward actually helps you to think more clearly. So give this backward walk through the last few minutes or hour of your life a try.

Nov. 12, 2009

Before I picked up my pen to write today, I stood at the kitchen counter and made a fruit salad. Before that, I leaned back in my chair and thought about the person whose hands picked the bowl of late summer cherries. Before that, I put on my Ugg boots and remembered the spider who mistook my bathtub for his home last night. Before that, I walked upstairs and ran my hand along the metal railing. Before that, I stopped and gazed out at the redwood trees and felt the cat weave between my feet. Before that, I checked the mail and watched a red-tailed hawk soar above my roof. Before that, I waved to my neighbor, Michelle, whose smile makes me smile. Before that, I pulled on my black sweater, shoved my hands into the pockets, and found a quarter. Before that, I searched for my favorite felt-tipped pen and wondered what time my Muse would arrive.

Your Turn

Create your own rewind of time.

Try This....

A Color Only My Soul Can Understand

A famous artist named Paul Klee said, "Color is the place where our brain and the universe meet." Colors are amazing—they speak every language; they show our moods, feelings, memories; describe physical surfaces like mountain tops and swimming pools, old barns, summer mornings, and baseball fields before dark. Pick a color. It might be your favorite color, or it might be a color you haven't worn or given much thought to in a while. Then take a walk. Take your time to see and feel *all* the things that are this color. Imagine your entire body as this color—inside and out—acting like a magnet, drawing everything that is this same "shade frequency" to you. Then find *your* answers to as many (or as few) of the questions below as you want. You might make up a new name or moniker for your color, like "Em-a-plo-va-zar." You might become an adventurer who's not afraid to wander *inside* the maze of nooks and crannies in every hue.

Em-a-plo-va-zar!

Em-a-plo-va-zar, a color made by me, is a mixture of maroon, pear, plum, aqua, topaz, and copper. A beautiful color only my soul can understand. It zips through my imagination and shoves all the other colors of my body, so it can deliver happiness and joy to my soul. It lopes around some days, so when I feel the slightest thing that makes me upset it can immediately come and cheer me up. It sways its cup of hot chocolate and tells stories to the other colors. It forces itself to crawl out of bed if something bothers me during the night. It has to be tough to withstand the murmuring and jealousy of the other colors. It is swollen with love for me. A square shape to stand out from all the other circular colors, it's curved inside for flexibility so it can move with ease around my body. "Pendelise," a shape of which I do not know, but it fits just the same, jutting and pointy to fight off all things I do not like.

—Molly

Our Friend, Blue

Blue's imagination is shaped like the sky.
Peacock feathers, lost buttons and the deep side of the ocean
are all part of blue's collection. At midnight,
Blue tiptoes across an indigo storm to swim Time's river.
Strong and tender, blue crosses to the other side
to count rainbows and sing songs about whales
dreaming and what it takes to create the world.
All of blue's secrets are kept in a box of friendship,
held together with a piece of string and a turquoise lid.

—group poem

Your Turn

How does your color move?

———————————————————————————————

In what season was it born?

———————————————————————————————

What place(s) does it take you?

———————————————————————————————

What time of day or night does it like?

———————————————————————————————

What does your color wish for?

———————————————————————————————

What is hidden behind it?

———————————————————————————————

What sound isn't your color?

———————————————————————————————

What 3 other things aren't your color?

———————————————————————————————

What is it a box of?

———————————————————————————————

What is it a song of?

———————————————————————————————

What is it the shape of?

———————————————————————————————

Who are its friends?

———————————————————————————————

Synesthesia or What Blue Sounds Like

Imagine if whenever you heard a bird's song or felt the wind through your hair, a shade of blue or a triangular pattern filled your brain. Syn-es-the-sia is when a person's senses are twisted or crossed. It's when you experience one sense *through* another. Some people with synesthesia see a specific color whenever they hear a particular sound. (Many artists and musicians have synesthesia.) A letter like *z* can cause a bright burst of red the color of apple skin to rush into their head. They might describe their cat's meow as a zigzagging orange. Or they might hear a high-pitched *whirl* or get a metallic taste in their mouth when they draw a series of circles.

Making up answers to these questions might help you spiral closer to understanding synesthesia and the different ways we all see and experience the many layers of our inner and outer worlds.

What color does a star sound like?   A star sounds like_____

What's the taste of a howl?   A howl tastes of_____

What is the smell of a circle?   A circle smells like_____

What color is a baby's cry?   A baby's cry is bright_____

How does white move?   White moves in a_____

What does a whisper look like?   A whisper looks like a_____

What does mischief smell like?   Mischief smells like_____

What is the texture of turquoise?   The texture of turquoise feels_____

What does a new idea feel like?   A new idea feels like_____

Answers from Kids Your Age

Blue sounds like the crack a glacier makes or the earth's heart-beat late at night.

The taste of a howl sits on my tongue and burns; sometimes it stings and makes my eyes water.

The smell of a circle is easy: it's a combination of wet pavement and chalk.

A baby's cry is definitely pink, a bright pink that refuses all other colors except white or gray.

White moves like my mother when she's happy to see me and my sister and hugs us close.

A whisper looks like a long shadow against a wall or a paper doll cut the wrong way 'round.

Turquoise feels smooth and cold and can't wait to be unfolded and warmed up like yellow.

A NOTE FROM: *Avi*

Dear Young Writer,

Everybody has ideas. The question is what do you do with them? My rock musician sons shape their ideas into music. My sister takes her ideas and fashions them into poems. My brother uses his ideas to help him understand science.

What do you think you'll do with your ideas?

I believe reading is the key to writing. The more you read, the better your writing can be. Listen and watch the world around you. Try to understand why things happen. Don't be satisfied with answers others give you. Don't assume that because everyone believes something, it is right or wrong. Reason things out for yourself. Work to get your answers on your own. Understand why you believe things. Finally, write what you honestly feel then learn from the criticism that will always come your way.

Your friend,

Avi

A Sample of Avi's Writing

FROM *Poppy*

It was as if the sun had been stolen. Only thin ribbons of light seeped down through the green and milk air, air syrupy with the scent of pine, huckleberry, and juniper. From the rolling, emerald-carpeted earth, fingers of lacy ferns curled up, above which the massive fir and pine trees stood, pillar-like, to support an invisible sky. Hovering over everything was a silence as deep as the trees were tall. Poppy gazed at it in awe. She was not sure what she'd thought Dimwood Forest would be like. She knew only that she'd never imagined it so vast, so dense, so dark. The sight made her feel immensely isolated and small. Feeling small made her a part of all she saw. Being part of it made her feel immense. It was terribly confusing.

Avi writes historical fiction, fantasies, comedies, mysteries, ghost stories, adventure tales, realistic fiction, and picture books. He has published 70 books written for children and young adults. His fiftieth book, Crispin: The Cross of Lead *was awarded the Newbery Medal in 2003.*

Whatever You Do, Don't Make Sense

Here's a dare. OK, a double dare. OK, a cross-your-heart-hope-to-die-stick-a-needle-in-your-eye dare. Bet you can't answer the following and *not* make sense. Try it. I dare you.

The opposite of tender is_____.

At the edge of silver is_____.

The sadness of puppies is_____.

At the center of boredom is_____.

At the top of tomorrow waits_____.

The swirl of loneliness sounds like_____.

The enemy of green hides between_____.

The shape of the past fits inside_____.

The rock bottom of October will never_____.

The antonym of pink is_____.

The hiding place of rain shivers underneath_____.

If you turn hope on high, you'll see_____.

If you look underneath peace, you might hear_____.

When you toss sadness to the wind, it returns as_____.

If you jump into the present, you'll land on_____.

When you tiptoe through the Valley of Happiness, you might find

_____.

A Moment of Life

At the top of tomorrow waits a gazing owl.
The edge of silver, I cannot describe.
Inside a startling bark is a roar.
When you tiptoe through the Valley of Happiness,
you might hear whispers of howling purple.
The shape of the past fits inside a droopy raindrop.
The enemy of green hides between a rocky waterfall.
If you look underneath peace, you might hear eager cries.
If you turn hope on high, you will find
the colorful starlight in the sky.

—Samantha

Your Turn

Triple dare: See if you can extend your sentences by using 10–20 words (or more . . .) or combine your favorite lines to make a poem like Samantha did.

GALLOPING CHIPPED GREEN

Try combining a shape and a movement with a color—to create a whole new look. *Flying, frilled brown. Tip-toeing, chubby lavender. Galloping chipped green. Swaying, slouching crimson. Slinky pointed cinnamon. . . .* How many different combinations can you string together?

MOVEMENT

hurry	run	skip	scramble	dart	spring
sprint	stride	trot	gallop	dash	bolt
rush	race	zip	speed	whisk	careen
shove	smash	drop	plummet	bounce	dive
swoop	fly	sail	crawl	plod	slouch
tiptoe	bend	amble	saunter	slink	stalk
stagger	lope	canter	waddle	sway	soar
drift	droop	swoop	lumber	swing	slink

SHAPES

flat	domed	curved	top-heavy	branching
scalloped	rotund	twiggy	broken	clustered
ruffled	lumpy	padded	frilled	jagged
tufted	tapering	triangular	globular	wavering
round	square	rectangular	chubby	shattered
oval	octagonal	wavy	jutting	pointy
swollen	starred	angular	pendulous	chipped

COLORS

RED	YELLOW	BLUE	BROWN	GREEN	WHITE
pink	beige	sky	sandy	mint	snow
salmon	mustard	sapphire	almond	apple	milky
rose	peach	azure	amber	lime	cream
coral	apricot	turquoise	tawny	emerald	ivory
raspberry	buttercup	aqua	cinnamon	olive	oyster
strawberry	gold	violet	copper	pistachio	pearl
crimson	orange	peacock	bronze	kelly	platinum
ruby	butterscotch	cobalt	walnut	chartreuse	eggshell

Sh@pe-Shifting

Last night I took flight through a maze of fallen tree limbs and clocks and deadlines and, feeling larger (and lighter) than before, I sashayed and shimmied while keeping my footing in mid-air. I came face-to-face with fire. I turned into a wolf. Then a sheep. Then into the soul of a tree. Each breath kept bringing me closer to the exact center of everything. My life unfolded into a surprise party of soothing lullabies, a friendly bandit, a row of corncobs, and unlocked doorknobs. I can't explain why, but I can now translate the left side of the sky. My arms have become the wings of a great white bird. My heart, the moon. Lowering back to earth, I stand firm, on my own two feet again. I wiggle each toe and unplug my clock radio, knowing this shape-sifting dream is only the beginning of all the ways I have learned to sing.

You change your clothes, your mind, your hair length, your underwear. So what about changing your shape? Become a tiger, a wave, a game of hopscotch, a kid in a spacesuit holding a star. When you shape-shift, you get to take a break from being you and borrow *all* the talents of something—or someone—else for a while. Shape-shifting is common in mythology, fantasy, and science fiction. You've probably already experienced shape-shifting if you remember your dreams, since dreams have a way of letting you become one thing one second, and something else the next. Sometimes all it takes is one strange image or tiny detail caught from the end of a dream to propel you into this kind of writing.

"And then I suddenly woke up," need not ever be written. Just start by looking at your own waking and dreaming life as a surprise party of ideas. You might walk through room after room, carrying a special searchlight that turns one thing into another. Who knows, you might discover your nightstand is a tollbooth; your reading glasses, two small icebergs. Look at your feet and hands—what have they become?

If you want to play at writing strange, then shape-shifting is definitely your game. Catch a dream by its tail and reel it back in. Make up what you can't remember. Have fun becoming everything (and everyone) you once might have been.

Your Turn

Different Dictionary

Here's a way to experiment with your own meaning of words and be the first to find out what your favorite noun or solid object feels like *from the inside*. Give it a try. Uncover what lives at the core of *how* a word means (*to you*). Put *Webster's* aside and define, define, define as you write inward toward the heart of a word's secret center. Seriously, don't go near the dictionary definition. Peel back the layers and arrive at your *own* private x-ray gaze of how a word really moves and grooves to everything trapped and humming deep inside.

mirror	*sunset*
two-way wall	not sunrise
shining through	not sun-sleep
your soul	but blunt colors
or an outer door	adjusting to the night
to your inner	fireworks facing off
life	when the ocean turns
	into a tangerine highway
	driving its light upon us

winter

white rabbit stillness
out of breath fog
iced over meadows
misty footprints
of peace
not napping owls
but a snowstorm's
journey home

calm

not the heat of tomorrow
not the moon of last night
but inside the outside
this heart of right now
not the humming of clocks
or trickle of water
but an upside down map
and ribbons of wind

Your Turn

Make your own definition poem.

Forget about punctuation.   Forget about complete sentences.

Forget about capitalization.   Remember you can begin your lines with *not*.

Dear Young Creative Writer,

I have a rebellious streak, and it comes out when I'm writing. I like to act like a mad chemist and put things together that don't normally mix, such as math and poetry. I like to mix science and poetry, too, so I write about the shapes in a spider web, the hexagons in a beehive, the angle created by migrating birds. I like to flip types of writing on their heads. When I write novels, I mess with the form. When I write haiku with writers in schools, sometimes we write "loose sound haiku," where we don't worry about the syllables being 5-7-5 and where one of the lines is a repeated sound. When I compile anthologies of teen writing, I look for poetry that takes risks with form, with language, and with the degree of honesty. If you like structure, great. It can be fun—like a puzzle. If you don't like structure, go ahead and rebel. Be a mad chemist. Take risks.

Experiment!

Betsy Franco

P.S. After writing my book *Mathematickles!,* I continued to write math poems that I call *mathematickles*. The ones below are about animals you might see on a walk.

A Sample of Betsy Franco's Writing

rooftops

porches

+ under cars

where the neighborhood kitties are

puddles – rescued worms = cloudy mirrors

potato bug x palm = sudden sphere

flocks ÷ autumnsky = migration R winter

Betsy Franco has spent a lot of her life writing poetry, and her greatest inspiration has been the limitless imaginations of her three creative sons. Her books include a collection of concrete poems, A Curious Collection of Cats *(Tricycle Press), a collection of two-voice poems,* Messing Around on the Monkey Bars *(Candlewick Press), and a book of math haiku that tickle your brain called* Mathematickles! *(Simon & Schuster).*

Haiku's Little Leap

A haiku is a short 3-line poem.

First line's *short* (some say 5 syllables short; others say short is just fine . . .)

Second line's *longer* (some say 7 syllables long; other say longer is just fine . . .)

Third line's *short again*

Think of a haiku as a little moment that tip-toes up to find you. A moment you capture *exactly* as you experience it, so the person reading your 3 lines *feels* the moment too, the same as you. The subject of haiku often contain small, un-important things that most people rush past and completely miss. Paw prints in the dirt. A broken spider web. The way sunlight lands on your cat's belly, or your dad's head. A tiny furled-up leaf. An owl's wings flapping. There's usually a lit-tle *ahhh* feeling that happens inside of you when you find or read a good haiku. It can feel like a calm flutter. Or an excited little leap.

My dad
bald on the top
getting older.
—Eric

A hedge of thorns—
how skillfully the dog
wriggled under it!
—Issa

An owl
flies toward the moon,
wings flapping.
—Collin

A grasshopper
chirps in the sleeve
of the scarecrow.
—Chigetsu

Pray,
think of a journey—
take one.
—Lucy

Under the trees
in the salad, into the soup—
cherry blossoms.
—Basho

Haiku Hints

Write what's happening in the moment.

Look for small details.

Don't explain—let your images do the talking.

Try speaking to—not about—your subject.

Let what's surprising or funny come last.

Rip the Page!

Pretend you're a fortune teller. With the assistance of scissors, turn this page into a pile of small rectangular strips and make some predictions—nice ones, never mean—like the kind you find inside Chinese fortune cookies. Add details with the help of similes and word lists. Here's one I made for my best friend, Lynn, *"You will slither through a happy life, side-winding your way to great success."* Tuck your made-up fortunes into places where they'll be found when you're not around: your mom's purse, your dad's empty coffee cup, your sister's coat pocket, a friend's lunch sack. . . . Write a few extra fortunes and leave them for someone you don't know to find: inside a book you return to the library; on a sidewalk, under a rock; tucked under the windshield wiper of a car . . .

Idioms

An *idiom* is a phrase (a group of words) that's been hanging out for so long together, it has become a team of words that means something different on the inside than how it reads on the outside. If you haven't heard a certain idiom before, you might scratch your head and say *huh?!?* Especially if you try to understand it *literally*. You have to live in the town or country where idioms are used to really get them. Idioms don't travel well. People in Spain use certain idioms that people in America probably wouldn't understand. An idiom used in Brazil would not make sense to a person from France. An *idiom* uses comparisons (you know, metaphors) to make simple ideas into images (pictures you see in your mind). You could say to your friend who cut his leg and claims he's bleeding to death, "Come on, Sam, don't exaggerate. You're not dying!" Or you could use an idiom, "Sam, *quit making a mountain out of a molehill*" (especially since his cut is just a scratch). Below are some popular idioms. Enjoy them, then go hunt for some of your own.

> You could say: "Mike is complaining about everything today." Or you could use the idiom: "Mike sure has a **bee in his bonnet** today."

> You could say, "Anna is so *not* sad. Her tears aren't real." Or you could use an idiom: "Faker!—those are **crocodile tears**!" (It's believed crocodiles weep before they eat their victims.)

You could say: "My dad is the greatest. He knows how to face a tough situation." Or you could use an idiom: "My dad's the greatest; he knows how to **take the bull by the horns**."

You could say: "Hey, Mom, Kiki's painting won first place!" If you're Kiki, that was your big news. You could use this idiom and say to your sister: "Hey, you **stole my thunder**."

You could say: "Natalie is not really a nice person. She just acts like she is." Or you could use an idiom and say, "Watch out! She's **a wolf in sheep's clothing**."

Try This....

Start With The Facts

Instead of writing the same old boring *How are you? I'm fine* type of letter to your favorite cousin, why not start by asking if she knows that the lifetime average spent talking is 10 years. Or that every person you love is 72.8 percent water (*slosh, slosh!*). Begin a piece of writing with a fun fact that will grab your readers' attention and stop them in their tracks, so they might scratch their heads and ask themselves, *Hmmmmm, let's see, you don't say? Is that a fact?* Memorizing a fun fact can also be a great conversation starter. Let's say you're standing there, the new kid at recess, wondering how to break the ice. Casually you ask if anyone can lick their own elbow. (You know it's impossible. They don't.) And before you make it to the front of the line, you have a group of new friends giving the elbow-lick a try. Pick a fact below that surprises you and use it to start a letter or jump-start a conversation. How many more little-known facts can you dig up?

The longest recorded flight of a chicken is 13 seconds.

A snail can sleep for 3 years.

A crocodile cannot stick out its tongue.

In a day, your foot can produce more than a pint of sweat.

You share your birthday with at least 9 million other people on Earth.

Cats have over 100 vocal sounds; dogs only have about 10.

There are more turkeys in California than in any other state.

The average 4-year-old asks over 400 questions a day.

The average weight of skin a person sheds in a lifetime is 40 lbs. (18 kg.).

Dolphins sleep with one eye open.

If you head-butt a soccer ball, you lose brain cells (unconfirmed).

Humpback whales are the only whales known to sing.

The albatross of Antarctica can go years without touching the ground.

The person you love is 72.8 percent water (worth saying again).

Your Turn

The Imagination's World Record

No doubt you've heard of the Guinness World Records, the book that keeps track of *all* the amazing record-breaking feats of who can carve a face into a pumpkin the fastest; who can sit in a bathtub with 87 rattlesnakes the longest; which group of kids can make the most snow angels simultaneously. There are *thousands* of categories and records that have been attempted and set. Except for this one. So how about letting your long and tireless Imagination compete? Take a chance. There's nothing to lose. All you have to do is enter a line or 2 in as many categories below as your imagination's prepared to win.

The Truest Thing	The Hardest Thing	The Flattest Thing
The Softest Thing	The Deepest Thing	The Noisiest Thing
The Most Difficult Thing	The Friendliest Thing	The Saddest Thing
The Highest Thing	The Kindest Thing	The Slowest Thing
The Bumpiest Thing	The Roundest Thing	The Happiest Thing
The Easiest Thing	The Stickiest Thing	The Funniest Thing

Maybe your Imagination will soon hold the record for the most *Things* it can dream up for categories. Or maybe you'll win for an individual line or group of lines. Keep going! You can do it! You're almost there!

The Imagination's Lines of World Records (Spoken Out-Loud by Students)

The highest thing is the blended voices of 12 baboons.

The bumpiest thing is a depressed pancake without maple syurp.

The friendliest thing is an undiagnosed dream.

The easiest thing is catching a tumbleweed on your tongue.

The quietest thing is unwrapping a mummy.

The slowest thing is a bruised snake.

Your Turn

Dear Writer,

Oh, there's a lot of advice in the world and I won't bother with all that. I'll just tell you what I tell myself: Be a storyteller, first and last. You want to know what happens when writers get together? They tell stories. That's really all they do.

The best writers talk a story the way they put it down on the page: the structure, the nuance, the beats, the language, the whole bag. Writers, you see, are always on the job, always practicing, always taking raw life and futzing with it, improving it by shaping it into a story. So practice your storytelling, not just on the page, but out loud. Practice over dinner. Be conscious of what you're saying, and watch your audience carefully. Are they leaning in? Are they excited? Or are they, God help you, bored? Observe the best storytellers you know—be it your mother or your soccer coach or your kid brother. Some of the best storytellers I've known happen to be children. They are deadly good, without an ounce of sentimentality.

The good ones instinctively know to arrive late and leave early in a story; they know to take the audience by the hand and never let go.

Best of luck to you!

Carol Edgarian

A Sample of Carol Edgarian's Writing

FROM *Rise the Euphrates*

He had his soccer ball tucked under his arm.

"Kick it," I said.

His eyes fluttered.

"Kick it," I said again.

The wind blew crystals off the tall pines. The party music pumped beneath our feet. He nodded once, or seemed to.

It happened so fast that afterward I could not be certain that he had moved. His body coiled and—*thunk*—the ball sailed up over the trees. We heard it land—*thunk*—way off in the neighbor's yard.

Adam BenKiki turned to look at me, displaying a row of perfect teeth.

There was not a word in my head. Not a word as he leaped over the railing and made off through the snow. He hopped over a hedge, and when he reached the ball he sat on his heels in the snow. He was like one of those ceramic leopards they put in yards to scare away the birds.

Carol Edgarian is the author of Rise the Euphrates *and other works of fiction and nonfiction. She's also the cofounder and editor of* Narrative Magazine *(www.narrativemagazine.com), which publishes stories, poems, cartoons, and art aimed at readers young and old.*

What Fits in Your Fist

Here's a starter list. Mix and match. Group them into 5, 10, 15, 20 . . . or as many as your hands, stories, and poems can hold. Use them for small details when making metaphors and similes. Add as many fist-sized objects as the wheelbarrow of your writing life can comfortably carry.

pen cap	ping-pong ball	guitar pick
grape	lemon	crayon
shark's tooth	hamster	bumble bee
dandelion fluff	raindrop	scoop of ice cream
ice cube	worm	maple leaf
apple moth	foxtail	marble
toenail	olive pit	orange wedge
eggshell	glass shard	golf ball
pearl earring	mosquito	gold medal
pebble	sock	sewing needle
daddy longlegs	diamond ring	fish
milk dud	walnut	fossil

shoe string	baby turtle	scorpion
rabbit's foot	marshmallow	radish
popcorn kernel	quarter	Barbie sunglasses
feather	black widow	bent straw
dust bunny	eraser	stamp
strawberry	wisp of cotton candy	thumb tack
dog tag	silver dollar	paper clip
tree frog	fingernail	cat's whisker
pancake	porcupine quill	mini rubber ducky
key	garlic bulb	twig
rubber band	paper airplane	deflated balloon
daffodil	snowball	snowflake
cockroach	butterfly	bottle cap

Something HUGE That Hurt

After the Divorce

The night our father left I found my sister in the living room, in front of the muted television screen. She was twirling her ponytail and asked me what we should do now. But the words on my tongue dissolved like cotton candy. Everything that happened—and was about to happen—was like a maze of loose spider webs I couldn't tame. I felt like a butterfly with one wing, so I did the only thing I could think of: I took my sister by the hand and led her down the hall into the bathroom. For a long time we just stood in front of the mirror, making sure we were both still there. And when she asked if she could sleep with me, I moved my pillow over and smoothed out the sheets. I didn't know how to explain that our father didn't want half of anything—not me, not her—that all he wanted was the two-lane road, taking him deeper into the fog of scotch and almond orchards.

Pick something that felt or still feels HUGE to you. It might be a HUGE feeling, like embarrassment: that time you spilled water on yourself at recess and everyone pointed and asked if you'd peed your pants. Or a HUGE problem: like when your best friend doesn't want to hang out with you. Or a HUGE memory: the night you overheard your parents talking about getting a divorce. Sometimes when you're writing about something HUGE—being made fun of, a thoughtless remark, the death of a pet, your parents' divorce—it helps to sprinkle in a handful of small things as you move your pen across the page, to support that great big HUGE thing, sitting in the center.

Your Turn

 Rip the Page!

Scars are part of life. At some point we all take a turn at falling down, and with bruised knees and scraped elbows, pick ourselves back up again. Sometimes we may need a few stitches or a long rest on the couch with our pillow and a plate of toast. Then weeks, months, years later, we have a scar to prove we have lived. Scars can be found on the outside AND on the inside of our bodies. Sometimes just the way a person speaks to us can cut at our heart and leave an invisible scar. Make your own scar-sketch. Tip the word S-C-A-R on its side and see what oozes out. Put your initials on it, date it, and tape it above your desk. Look in the mirror and congratulate yourself. Smile at that brave warrior gazing back at you.

In Praise of Odes

The word *ode* is from a Greek word meaning *song*. An ode is a poem of praise where you get to say—or sing—everything you like or love about someone or something. The tone, how your voice sounds in the poem, is kind, generous, and enthusiastic. The famous Chilean poet, Pablo Neruda, wrote an entire book of Odes called *Odes to Common Things*, where he praised ordinary objects, including a pair of scissors, a bar of soap, a cluster of violets, a violin in California, French fries, even a pair of socks. You get the idea: you can write an ode to *anything*. Yes, even to your belly; even to your hands.

Oh, Beautiful Belly

Oh, beautiful belly,
Bless yourself.
Rejoice! Remember:
bagels,
breathing,
babies,
bed,
Botticelli,
Bali,
breakfast,

bon-bons,
bright blue balloons,
broccoli,
Beethoven,
Basho,
Baudelaire,
Bo Diddley,
Big Bird,
Bee-bop-a-loo-bop,
Bee-deedley-doo,
Bingo.

—Linda Wolfe

Ode to My Hands

Black bats
bright pink pine forests
purple snakes
orange creeks
yellow twigs
indigo lights
white electricity
lavender lightning
silver feathers
gold ears of animals
are my hands.

—Kirsty

What part of your body will you write an ode to?

Try This. . . .

Stop Time

The poet Charles Simic believes "the secret wish of poetry is to stop time." So what if tomorrow you wake up, roll over, check the clock, and instead of 6 a.m. flashing back, poetry's wish has—*yikes!*—come true? In the middle of the night, all the numbers in the world have disappeared. Now *the-hour-we-all-come-back*, is flashing back at you. No more 7 a.m. Instead, it's *hour of-the-cat-at-the-door*. 8 a.m. has vanished, too, and in its place is the *hour-of-apricot-light.* All the numbers in every town, state, province, country, bus schedule, math test, worksheet, wristwatch, cell phone, and calculator have, *poof,* disappeared into a thick white haze. In the beginning, things feel a little crazy. But then everyone starts to get used to their new numberless way of living. There's *hour-that-looks-out-on-all-the-others. Beating-heart-hour. Meet-you-on-the-blacktop-after-school-hour. Take-a-shower-and-read-a-chapter-hour. Snuggle-down-beneath-the-moonlight-hour.* You get the idea.

Favorite Hour

It's the hour of stars twirling
and tornados tumbling out of reach—
The hour the sun swallows the sky
and luck runs up panting, eating a peach.
The hour when tiny wishes tuck themselves

163

on either side of the horizon's thin arms,
and no one cares about wasting time or worrying
about what is or isn't yours, his, hers or mine.
The hour when each *Open Sesame* you dare to speak
carries you deeper into the spiraled center
where the world's heart beat enters you mind.

—Katrina Trelawny

Your Turn

All the numbers have crawled into hibernation. As newly-appointed
Keeper of the Hours, you're left to rename each one, and decide what
defines your sense of time. Ideas include:

Arranging 12 lines of sentence fragments to create a new clock face.
Adding dashes between the words of your favorite hour-name-words.
Making your own "Favorite Hour" poem.

Notice What You Notice

Between Luck & Loneliness

I'm in Los Angeles, for my friend Joni's wedding. It's half past 5 in the evening and the sky is starting to slide into pink. I'm alone in the hotel room, writing. The air conditioner was left on all day— it's so cold I have *Titanic* toes. They're all huddled inside my socks. The desk, black with a glass top, makes me miss my wooden desk at home. There's a dead fly on the windowsill. My tongue's thirsty for crushed ice and lemonade. The lampshade is a parallelogram, off kilter on its base. Half a banana with brown spots rests on a copy of *Frindle* by Andrew Clements. The person next door must be moving a piano. My pencil has a blue eraser that smudges. The painting above the desk is of a lily pad. The artist signed his name all squiggly; the only letter I recognize is "J." There are 4 clouds in the sky. My heart keeps beating between luck and loneliness. I have to get dressed soon, though I wish I could stay in my pajamas forever. I brush the fly out the window, take off my socks, and leave my pen to rest on the desk. I'm in Los Angeles, with 4 clouds and 10 cold toes, leaving soon for my friend Joni's wedding.

So what are you doing, or about to be doing? Maybe you're counting your teeth. Maybe you're about to put a straw in a chocolate milkshake or pedal off on your bike down a tree-lined street. Wherever you are, whatever you're doing—or are about to be doing—stop and look around. Right now. What do you see? Write down *everything*. After living on Earth longer than 5 years, we stop noticing what we notice. This is NO RULES WRITING. You can write in broken bits of thought. You can go back and forth between what you notice on the outside (furniture-moving sounds) and what you notice on the inside (that thirsty feeling on your tongue). Tune in to what you see, hear, smell, taste, feel. Become a reporter of your life. Get interested at what's in front of your nose and touching the edge of your toes. If you can do this, there's a good chance you'll rediscover *everything* as fresh, new, simple, brilliant, *and* inspiring. Make a circle and end your writing the same way you started.

Your Turn

Dear Young Writer,

I started writing because I had an idea for a story and I wanted to know what happened. I wanted to know about the character and what her life was like, and the only way I could do that was to make it up and write it down. When I think of my writing like that now, it seems easy and brings me great joy. When I think, "Oh, I have to write a *whole* book!" or "Will readers, teachers, booksellers, librarians *like* this book I am writing?" or "This *has* to be good, better, the best book of all!" the joy goes away. The best reason to write is just to find out what happens.

Love,
Karen

A Sample of Karen Cushman's Writing

FROM *Alchemy and Meggy Swann*

"Ye toads and vipers," the girl said, as her granny often had, "ye toads and vipers," and she snuffled a great snuffle that echoed in the empty room. She was alone in the strange, dark, cold, skinny house. The carter who had trundled her to London between baskets of cabbage and sacks of flour had gone home to his porridge and his beer. The flop-haired boy in the brown doublet who had shown her a straw-stuffed pallet to sleep on had left for his own lodgings. And the tall, peevish-looking man who had called her to London but did not want her had wrapped his disappointment around him like a cloak and disappeared up the dark stairway, fie upon him! Fie upon them all!

Karen Cushman is the author of The Midwife's Apprentice, *winner of the 1996 Newbery Medal,* Catherine Called Birdy, *a Newbery Honor book,* The Ballad of Lucy Whipple, *winner of the John and Patricia Beatty Award, and several other prize-winning novels published by Clarion Books. Her newest book is* Alchemy and Meggy Swann. *Karen lives and writes on Vashon Island in Washington state.*

Rip the Page!

Don't touch this page until you're in a red-hot, steaming fiery-FURY. About to fly-off-the-handle-bars ticked-off, can't see straight CRAZY. Ready to slam a door, punch a wall, shred a pillow, and CHEW the feathers off a live chicken. Then reach for a pencil, break it in half, and write THROUGH YOUR RAGE. Go on, really give it to the page. Don't hold back. Race ahead of any thoughts that say, *Aw, come on, that's not very nice.* Include ALL your thoughts and feelings. Everything you want to SCREAM . . . to EVERYONE you want to yell at. Scrawl your heart out. Then DESTROY this page (rip, tear, crumble, chew); or use a hole punch until it looks like Swiss cheese.

Z to A

A *always* gets to be first in line. While Z runs up, arriving last again. Circle 26 words, one for each letter of the alphabet, to use for a silly story that doesn't have to make sense. Squeeze more words into the white space below; let any words you like cut to the front of the line.

zipper	trapeze	nail	icicle	drool
zany	twirl	nephew	inch	daffodil
zigzag	trinket	niece	hush	catapult
yowl	starfish	mushy	helmet	cursive
yoga	skitter	murmur	howl	crawl
yacht	swarm	muddy	guppy	create
x-ray	reef	lucky	gravity	blaze
X-mas	riddle	ladder	goggles	bundle
wild	raincoat	lamp	goat	bon-bons
whack	race	lost	flute	burrow
wrinkle	quilt	kite	fence	balance
walrus	quiver	kayak	fork	bridge
voodoo	promise	kitchen	epic	anxious
vortex	pinball	jazz	extinct	anteater
villain	plank	jungle	elevator	alarm
ukulele	organ	jet	driftwood	about-face

Seek the Hiding

The vowels are missing, and *you* have to find them. Where will you look for *a e i o u?* And what about *y* and *w?* These vowels, they're a cagey bunch. The only clue they've left is that they're *not* hiding together but have scattered in different directions. Where do you start? They can be *anywhere.* Before *w* left, he teased, "you'll never find me." *Y* yelled, "Don't waste your time!" They obviously don't know who they're dealing with. They haven't heard how determined you are, that you'll *never* give up. The rest of the alphabet is counting on you to get them out of this fix. Here's the note the vowels left. (Without *a e i o u,* it's hard to understand.)

"Cnt t 23 . . . nd scrm, *rdy r nt hr cm!*"

Translation: "Count to 23 and scream, *ready or not, here I come!*"

Clues to Some Possible Hiding Places

In a blade of wheat, behind a smile, around the bend, caught in the past, trapped inside winter, across the aisle from summer, in the middle of autumn, at the beginning of time, between drops of rain, caught in a daydream, under a rainbow,

deep in a pocket, near the end of the road, under the ocean,
taking a nap in somebody's lap.

I looked for *A* in the hollow of a tree
where the rope swing sways,
down at the creek where Nick and Collie play.
I searched inside the wind, behind the clouds,
between hours and numbers and on the backs
of little-known facts. I scanned the markings of zebras
and peered at the codes within a butterfly's wings.
I was ready to say, *Aw, just forget it; I give up* . . .
when I spotted *A* curled in lower case, snoring,
taking a nap in my great nana's lap. *Hey,* I yelled,
Scoot over! That's where I get to sleep.

Your Turn

I looked for A. . . .

___ _ _ ___ _ _ _ _ _ _ _ _ _ ___ _ _ _ _ _ _ _ _

I looked for E. . . .

_ _

I looked for I. . . .

_ _

I looked for O. . . .

_ _

I looked for U. . . .

_ _

Only Your
Nose Knows

Start wherever you are and follow each smell-combination to its source. With as much detail as you can provide, count your steps *back* to a particular smell's origin.

> This morning, I followed the smell of early morning skunk:
> Steps 1–3: across the bedroom, into my flip-flops, and out the open window . . .
> Steps 3–24: down the gnarled oak branch by bumpy branch . . .
> Steps 25–99: out the gate and up along the muddy deer trail . . .
> Steps 99–156: across the footbridge and through the woods . . .
> Steps 156–274: into tall grass for a peek inside that hollow log . . .
> Steps 274–280: *hey, what's with the raised tail . . . ?*

Your Turn

Choose a smell from the list and trace it from where you're sitting to its origin. It's OK to make up parts of your journey, if you like. Some smells might naturally lead to other smells.

early morning skunk spray

sweaty socks (left in a duffel bag all weekend)

roses (and bees)

chlorine mixed with coconut sunscreen

pumpkin pie and roast turkey

ripe apples (soon-to-be-pie)

clean sleeping baby

hay and horses

maple syrup and pancakes

shaving cream

wet dog (or cat)

pine trees and snow

fish (and crying seagulls)

popcorn and butter

sawdust

just–mowed grass

cinnamon toast

rain on hot pavement

lavender

woodsmoke

What other smells (or smell combinations) are there?

Personification Party

Personification is a way of giving things that *aren't* human—objects, natural colors, ideas, feelings, animals—human qualities, abilities, clothes, parents, friends, hobbies, and even opinions. Basically *anything* that you have, can do, or enjoy as a kid—sing, run, laugh, swim, blush, ride a bike, toss a Frisbee, eat a peach—you can loan to a particular color, like red. Or to the Quality of Love. Or even to the Ocean, the Rain, or last night's Thunderstorm. Personification is an act of generosity. You're breathing a little bit of your life—and imagination—into something non-human and sharing some of the gifts you were born with.

For example, here's what happened at a party when the colors showed up *personified,* and a poem about what the rain would be like if it were a fisherman.

Personification Party

Yellow was late. Orange drank two cups of soy sauce, mistaking it for soda. Blue whispered, "What a mess!" Red didn't talk much. White was busy with her soul. Green worried she'd make a mistake. Pink was lounging by the pool, tanning. Brown offered to help pay for the food. Gray was slow to answer. Black made them laugh.

Purple was shy and hid in the hollow of a tree and blushed when Blue called her to come down. Green was scared of Blue. Orange wasn't lying when she said she'd had a good time. Purple felt big drops of rain. Red handed out umbrellas. White said no thank you because she wanted to get wet.

—Gracie

Rain

Rain has no manners.
He creeps up on you, turning
everything as limp and damp
as a newborn bat's wings.
He's a fisherman in a dark
raincoat, dragging home
his catch of silver trout,
grumbling all the way.
He paints the world black
so he's the only light.

—Kyle

A NOTE FROM: *Patricia Polacco*

Dear Young Writer,

Who would have guessed that the little girl who was me that was having such a tough time in school would end up an author AND an illustrator? People ask me where I get my ideas. . . . I get them the same place you do. MY IMAGINATION. I would guess the reason my imagination is so fertile is because I came from a storytelling family, and WE DID NOT OWN A TV!!! You see, when one is a writer, actor, dancer, musician, creator of any kind, you write, act, dance, play music, and create things because you *listen* to that "voice" inside of you. All of us have that "voice." It's where all inspired thoughts come from. But when you have electronic screens in front of you, speaking that voice for you . . . IT DROWNS OUT THE VOICE! So turn off the TV and LISTEN . . . LISTEN . . . LISTEN.

Much love,
Patricia Polacco

A Sample of Patricia Polacco's Writing

FROM *The Graves Family Goes Camping*

Dr. Graves, knowing that it was nearly time to leave for the annual family camping trip, was desperately searching his shelves for just the right map. Now he climbed a tall ladder and pulled the dusty ancient scroll from the highest shelf. "Here it is!" he announced as he blew clouds of dust from the parchment and rolled it out on the desk.

Ronnie and his best friends, Seth and Sara, along with the family spiders, leaned over the map with great interest as Dr. Graves traced the map with his finger.

"There it is . . . Lake Bleakmire," he called out.

"And no one knows it's there but us, Dad?" Ronnie asked quietly.

"Almost no one," Dr. Graves answered, lost in thought. "Surrounded by a rocky escarpment with only one hidden tunnel leading thorough it, it is a place that time has forgotten. Untouched! A place legends are made of.

"Oh, children, just think what we might find there: new species of spiders, giant swamp leeches, even the warty *Toadus uglycus*. And," his voice dropped to a whisper, "perhaps creatures for which we have no names."

When not frightening the neighbors or creating new picture books, Patricia Polacco loves to travel around the country sharing her stories with children and speaking at school conferences, libraries, and bookstores. Some of her books include Thank You, Mr. Falker; Mrs. Katz and Tush; My Rotten Redheaded Older Brother; Picnic at Mudsock Meadow; Pink and Say; *and* Mrs. Mack.

 **Rip the Page!**

It's a little-known fact that it's harder to kill a spider hanging out in the bathtub if you've named him *Sammy*. Naming things—from spiders to swivel chairs—can be fun. Give it a try. *Jeffrey Jeep, Swivel Chair Charlie, Lucy Eucalyptus*, once just a seed from Australia who lost her way. Name five things—living or non-living—around your house. Space them out on this page then make name tags for your new pals. Introduce them to the people you live with, so they can get to know—and grow to love—them too.

Try This....

Catching Whispers

Everything has a sound, a voice, something that longs to be heard. But so often we don't get quiet enough to hear these sound-messages that the quietest things—trees, pebbles, mountaintops, clouds, spiders—share with us. In order to hear at this level, you must let your entire body—inside and outside—settle and land. It helps to be in a forest or near the ocean. But if there's not a forest handy or an ocean nearby, take a walk in a garden . . . or around your house with the windows open wide. (Desks, lamps, chairs, windowsills, plates, forks, knives, and spoons all have secrets to share, too.) Stand on a hill or up on a table. Sit in a patch of soft grass, or deep in the hollow of an old comfy couch. Even under your bed, or near one of those open windows will do. Then wait. Not an impatient kind of wait, but a gentle and relaxed being-in-the-no-where-else sort of receiving. Pretty soon, you'll hear it: all the sounds that were made from one distant sound; all the sounds that swirl *beneath* the whispered world. If you come back this time tomorrow, each thing you hear from today will have something new to say.

Your Turn

What do you hear? Finish the sentences below. (Hint: you might want to keep a word list near.)

Today, a cloud said . . .

———————————————————————————

Last night, a spider admitted . . .

———————————————————————————

The weeds pushing through the sidewalk asked if . . .

———————————————————————————

A bird flying over my roof sent down this wish . . .

———————————————————————————

A leaf on its way to the ground revealed . . .

———————————————————————————

Each doorknob keeps asking whether . . .

———————————————————————————

The hangers in my closet are wondering if . . .

———————————————————————————

What the spoon really wants to know is . . .

———————————————————————————

A mushroom tunneled up to sing . . .

———————————————————————————

The fireplace is begging to . . .

———————————————————————————

The tallest tree out back insists that . . .

———————————————————————————

A star just beamed me this message . . .

———————————————————————————

Gross-out Words

Sometimes you need a word that makes your sentences squirm. It could be a made-up word that ends in "-ish" or "-ified," to help you to express something truly icky or downright disgusting. Proceed with caution when using gross-out words. A few of these go a *long* way. Find out how fast you can create a feeling of feverish fly-infested welt-like fear for your unsuspecting reader. Enjoy!

belchified	garbage-like	greenish	maggot	crud-like
floppish	gunky	barf-like	rotting	oozing
darkish	slime	slimified	dandruff	crusty
scab-like	bloodsucker	mushified	lima beans	gooey
feverish	cockroach	gnaw	stickyish	hottish
pond scum	hurling	fly-infested	squirmish	mucus-like
sludgified	gagified	cesspool-like	sludge	sewer-like
swampy	hairy	vomit	liverwurst	lumpy
chug-a-lugified	sloshified	intestines	lumpy	welt-like
stinkified	scaly	mosquito bite	trashified	blob-like
squirmish	chicken pox–like	gunky	nodule	booger-like
leechish	flushified	wartish	cold sore	ear wax
spongy	mucus	leech-like	clumpy	flea-like
lumpy	slither-like	slimy	toe jam	moldified
saliva	diaperish	mildewish	bloodshot	liceified

How Much Fun Can You Have?

Have you ever stopped to consider how much fun you can have? Don't worry if what you're writing is impossible, rude, untrue, too scary, wearing the wrong kind of jeans, almost didn't happen, or is maybe a tad-bit green. It's OK if what's fun to you would make your Grandma Betty jump up and scream. Just jot down some fearless, free-flowing, how-much-fun-can-you-have-real-life-memories or daydreams. It's fine if they're combined from different ages and time zones. Let each sentence begin with an out-of-breath "And," like the example below. Jot down every detail without giving F-U-N a rest.

It Was Sooooo Fun

And we got to jump off these super-high rocks and splash-land in a deep cold creek. And it was freeeezing. And then Eliza's mom let us run outside and inside and outside and we didn't have to close the doors. And the boys all chased us. And we screamed and hid in Eliza's closet and covered our mouths so they wouldn't hear us laugh. And the boys never found us. And it was so fun because it started to snow! And the hill across the street was covered with powder. And we hiked to the top with cardboard squares and went sliding down on our butts. And it sounded like this—*sha-whooosh!*

And the wind was blowing in our faces as we raced to the bottom. And, guess what? I won! And then we started digging a snow-hole to China. And it was so fun because my mom let us stay up super-late. And later we got to make forts with pillows and cushions and blankets and sheets. And I got to invite Kristin Laymon over for a slumber party. And Betsy and Gina and Nikki and Krissy and Paisley and Rhoan and Ali and Dawnie came too. And all of us crammed into the downstairs family room at 345 Gordon Avenue. And we arranged our sleeping bags in a circle and ate popcorn and told ghost stories. And when my mom walked downstairs, we pretended to be sleeping. And then Rhoan whispered, "Great balls of fire!" And we couldn't fake it anymore. And then someone snorted (I think it was me). And we all laughed. And laughed.

Your Turn

Port Man Toe

Portmanteau is a French word for a "traveling bag" or "large suitcase." It's also what you end up with when you knit together the sounds and meanings of two words, like brunch (breakfast + lunch). Unpack your word suitcase and mix and match favorite words to create your own portmanteau words. They can be real words or nonsense words. Are there two words hanging in the closet of your imagination that want to be sewn together? Be as silly and serious . . . or *silerous* as you want. Your portmanteau words might be found in the dictionary. Or they might be made-up words, like the way Lewis Carroll, who wrote *Through the Looking Glass* and the fun-to-read poem *Jabberwocky,* created his own portmanteau words: like *slivy* and *mimsy.*

Here are some real portmanteau words mixed with some made-up ones.

smoke + fog = smog

chuckle + snort = chortle

mist + drizzle = mizzle

fantastic + fabulous = fantabulous

gigantic + enormous = ginormous

slimy + live = slivy

miserable + flimsy = mimsy

spoon + fork = spork

skirt + short = skort

play + work = plork

walk + marathon = walkathon

shirt + sleeve = sheeve

labrador + poodle = labradoodle

tiger + lion = tigon

vampire + giant = vamiant

fake + vacation = facation

Map Your Journey

The English archaeologist Howard Carter kept digging for years (and years) even though many people in Egypt said he'd *never* find the Tomb of Tutankhamen in the Valley of the Kings. Carter was determined though. He made detailed maps for himself that he marked off in triangular grids. And though he had a lot of help digging through all that sand and rubble, he was the one who had to keep his hope and belief alive, deep inside. Late at night, making his maps, he was the one who had to convince himself that it was worth continuing on, in search of the lost pharaoh.

Sometimes to find your way through uncertain or challenging times, and to get to the treasure you know is waiting for you, it helps to create a little map for yourself. Take it step by step. Leave no stone unturned. Chart your way among real *and* imaginary realms. And remember, the treasure you seek is also found within every moment along the way. Here are some words to begin each step of your quest: *begin, slide, turn, watch, proceed, ask, dig, climb, swim, find . . .*

Map to Treasure

Begin at the root where the black crow eats
Slide onto Huckaloo Trail
Back-flip until you hit the rock of pain
Turn right and climb up to Snowy Peak
Watch out for the angry hermit
Proceed with caution southeast for two miles
Ask the wind to erase your footprints
Dig through the pile of steaming dirt
End up at a creek filled with salmon
Put on the blue goggles waiting for you
Swim to the bottom and dig through soft mud
Soon you will find the silver and gold
Answers to the mysteries of your life.

—Alex

Your Turn

A NOTE FROM: *Prartho Sereno*

Dear Wizard-in-Training,

There's no end to the mystery of words. How is it that sounds from my mouth, throat, and lungs can send a story to you? I can give you the gold of the morning sky, the taste of a ripe strawberry, the smell of cinnamon toast, the *plunk* of a pebble tossed into a pond, the warm air of a summer night. I *love* the pictures words paint inside us. And I especially like to write about things I don't quite understand—any thing or person that seems mysterious to me.

Love,
Prartho

A Sample of Prartho Sereno's Writing

My Poem

My poem is a continent out beyond my brain;
My poem resounds with a slow fine rain,
a hurricane, a wagon train, a girl from Maine,
and the soft refrain of mynah birds and grateful words,
things unsaid and things unheard.

My poem is lit with fireflies, my poem arrives
with dampened eyes, just before all reason dies.

Inside my poem it's autumn night with geese in flight
and golden light. In the streets the people dance,
they take a chance, they end the trance,
believe in the power of a glance.

At the edge of my poem's a dragonfly, a samurai,
a hole in the sky, you and I, eye-to-eye,
out beyond the question why.
My poem is a continent out beyond my brain
where nothing is for worrying and no one is to blame.

Prartho Sereno is a painter and poet who recently was awarded an MFA fellowship from Syracuse University. The author of three books, including one she wrote and illustrated, Causing a Stir: The Secret Lives and Loves of Kitchen Utensils *(Mansarovar Press, 2007), she divides her time between New York and California and believes that second graders are the true mystics.*

Suddenly a Story . . . .

Real-Life Magic

I started practicing real-life magic in third grade and became an expert by the following summer. Whenever there was something I really wanted to have or to have happen—and I was *really* wishing and hoping hard—all I had to do was reach out for a handful of magic from deep inside the universe's endless supply. Somehow I knew this type of magic had nothing to do with pulling a rabbit out of a hat, and everything to do with believing in the everyday, ordinary magic that always seemed to be revealing itself to me. (I just figured it was the same for everybody—and now I know it is . . . if we can all just wake up long enough to notice!)

So one day, I decided to create what I wanted. I found a magic pillowcase from the upstairs linen closet, then found 5 small objects to drop inside—I chose a rock, a feather, a pinecone, a leaf, and an ice cube. (The ice cube magically disappeared, so I replaced it with a shell.) Then I wrote down 5 things I wanted on little scraps of binder paper. Three of these things I remember clearly. They were: having a slumber party with my best friends, Kristin Laymon and Gina Langone; taking a camping trip to Big Sur with my family; and hearing my mom say, "Sure, why not?" when I asked if I could get my ears pierced. Then I sat cross-legged in the center of my bed and, like a sorcerer who can change one thing into another, I reached inside my magic pillowcase, pulled out my rock, and turned it into that camping trip to Big Sur. I saw

194

the entire trip, as if it had already happened—me and my sister skipping stones with our father down at the oak-shaded creek; roasting marshmallows on long whittled sticks in front of the fire pit, stars pulsing and falling around us. I even made up a magic spell about how that rock would magically transport me and my family back to the gorge, deep in the heart of Phieffer Big Sur State Park.

To perform any act of real-life magic, you *must* be willing to walk the tightrope of true believing. You must hold back *all* doubt (also known in some magic circles as fear) and simply balance out, into your tiniest or wildest, most sought-after dream. Sometimes what you most long for has no other choice but to materialize and come true.

Later that summer, my father surprised us with a two-week camping trip to . . . (I already knew) Big Sur, where we got to pitch our tent at the site closest to the gorge and fall asleep to the sound of water rushing over stones. It was also the summer my mom let me invite 2 friends to spend the night *and* gave my aunt permission to take me to the mall, where a tiny hole was made in each ear then closed with gold.

Your Turn

What kind of everyday magic will you use to make your real-life dreams come true? If you're not sure, find a magic pillowcase and drop 5 small objects inside. Then go sit somewhere with this book and a pen, and write down 5 things you want to have or have happen. Write *in detail*. Don't worry about sentences or structure. Magic only cares about the depth of your imagination and the truth in your heart.

NOTE: Your magic might not take hold overnight but, if what you want is true enough (and longed-for with enough detail), something will shift. Just be open for what you want to come true to appear in a slightly different form than how you first imagined it. And remember to breathe!

States of Being

Make a friend with one of the words below and ask your new word-friend what it's most interested in and curious about. Jump around the way friends do. Let one question lead to another. Make friends with Laughter, Faith, Anger, or Wisdom and find out the answers to these questions: Where do you live? Who's your teacher? What's your favorite subject? Sport? What do you like to eat for lunch? What do you want to be when you grow up? What's your biggest problem? Where do you like to travel? What's your favorite instrument? Who do you talk to? What makes you laugh? Do you ever hide? What scares you? Do you have any brothers or sisters? What are their names? When's your birthday? When do you get your braces off? What's your favorite season? Color? Shape? Number? Song? Book? Place to hang out?

Silliness	Forgiveness	Calm	Compassion
Love	Hunger	Generosity	Terror
Absence	Loss	Excitement	Imagination
Stinginess	Fear	Stillness	Snobbery
Bravery	Doubt	Tenderness	Pride
Loneliness	Caution	Intensity	Wisdom
Peace	Happiness	Care	Disgust
Gentleness	Moodiness	Anxiety	Power

Respect   Creativity   Beauty   Amazement
Trust   Appreciation   Confidence   Embarrassment
Sadness   Joy   Anger   Shame
Imagination   Surprise   Nervousness   Faith

Faith

Faith, with her long brown hair,
wears an amethyst necklace.
She sings when the moon is full
as the wind drags the snow behind her.
October is Faith's tenth birthday.
She invites her best friends, Hope and Love,
Trust and her little sister, Truth.
Together, they have a party
in the center of dark blue.

—Laudi

Anger

Nobody likes him. Nobody notices him.
He can't be understood and is harsh
because of past memories. He has the stigma
of being unapproachable. When he's criticized,
he can't express himself. He wants to hide,
to disappear, to make it better . . .
How? Why? Can I? he asks himself.
Dark and hunched, he walks away.
He wears black and is scared to show his face.

—Abby

Your Turn

Sketch out a little stanza based on your new word-friend.

Running the Margin

My annoying sister/brother . . .

Winning a game . . .

A far-away memory . . .

That time I fell . . .

Running the Margin is the easiest thing to do *after* you know what you want to write about, but still aren't sure how to begin. Simply write your subject at the top of your margin . . . and roll down all the related words that come to you, as fast as you can. Write any old or young word that drifts, pops, or parachutes into your head. Don't stop to wonder why you wrote "Aunt Ella" when your subject is *prehistoric bone*. Maybe someone's Aunt Ella broke her arm while wrestling. Maybe someone knows a chicken named Aunt Ella. It just doesn't matter! All you care about is running that margin, lightning-fast, top to bottom. Whatever way you feel your margin-running words relate to your subject is the right way. Remember, *you're* the authority of your life. Ready, set. *Go!*

Here's how I used one of my memories to run the margin. First I came up with a subject: that time I fell into the rosebushes before kindergarten. Next, I wrote a list of words lickety-split in the margin, any word that I associated with that morning. Then, when I started to write about my fall, I had a list of words to help me along.

Late May Memory

Rosebushes

Bicycle

Blood

Bees

Yellow sweater

Patio

Upstairs

Front wheel

Dad

Mom

Thorns

School

Window

Pillow

Home

Kiss

Forehead

In a yellow sweater, I'm riding my bike before school, pedaling fast. I'm close to the edge of the patio where the roses are in bloom. I've forgotten all about thorns and my mother's warning to stay away from the stairs. My front wheel disappears first. It happens so fast. One second I'm on my bicycle seat, ringing my silver bell, and the next time I look up I'm hanging out with the bees. Thorns push their way into my skin. I cry out. My father's arms circle around me. The blood and scratch marks on my legs remind me of the lines from the paper I'm learning to print my name on. I'm carried upstairs to the bathroom where I feel the sting of Bactine. A square of blue sky huddles against my bedroom window as my parents' hushed voices in the next room discuss if they should *keep me home from school.* My heart soars. I love staying home! I make my smile disappear when I hear their footfall down the hall. "You've been so brave," my mother whispers. She brushes her fingers through my tangled hair and kisses my forehead. "But Daddy thinks you're alright to go to school."

Your Turn

Come up with a subject.

Run your pen down the page, word by word, sloppy and choppy.

Push ahead of your thoughts.

Relax. You don't have to explain or defend yourself.

Write a memory, poem, or story using your words.

Rip the Page!

Write your name in 5 different ways in the middle of the page (backward, upside down, right to left, left to right, with eyes closed). Then write the names of friends, family members, and cool grown-ups around the outside edge. In different colors, include a symbol (a spiral, a musical note, a peace sign, a lightning bolt, a heart, a star, a shamrock) or whatever doodle first pops or bursts on to the page. "First thought, best thought," said a wise trickster-poet named Chögyam Trungpa Rinpoche. After all your symbols and doodles are recorded, tear up a piece of this page and like a dandelion wish-weed, blow some tiny scraps into the wind (the paper was once a tree and is recyclable).

Leaping-off Lines

Some days when you're writing, you might get stuck at the top. Other days you might not feel strong enough to push off from the bottom. There might be a day you feel lost in the middle, want to change direction or shake up your writing routine. If this ever happens to you, it's time to borrow a line, fill up each squishy lung and jump-start your stalled imagination. Cut out the fragments below. Toss them into a hat. Play with them however, wherever, whenever you want.

knotted up	loose as pajamas	she leans across to
at your house	like a few wrinkles	like a seashell
she swoons	keep a secret	like a stone
he counts birds	twitches and cries out	wishbone of
like a butterfly	just for a second	he forgets his name
at breakfast	like a parakeet	latch clicks closed
with bean sprouts	quiet hands	peas and cucumbers
evening sun	like harbor lights	sand up to our knees
whirl upon whirl	at the edge of the path	carving a valley of

I burn past the

a power line falls

I face the camera

so this dog wears

high as barn rafters

skims the floor like

tomato vines

singing a song with

this past winter

catch the light

a train whistle, then

first one bootstrap, then

outside, shimmering blue

my sister squints

into stars

screech owl

bagpipes of

quick paws chase

a slow collapse of words

boxes of leaves

all around, flat land

against a sharp light

inside Grandma's arms

after the thunderstorm

tucked inside a suitcase

like a tiny red apple

it was only a trick

places we understand

he's narrowing down

like a slanting roof

Who's Your Muse?

A *Muse* is someone—or something—imaginary or very real, who gives you inspiration and helps your creativity flow like a clear stream through your pen. You can ask your Muse for something you need by using your "inner voice," but you have to stay "tuned in" in order to hear what she (or he) has to say. A Muse is *never* bossy or mean. A Muse simply sends you messages that arrive at odd moments, like when you're in the shower or sleeping or lost in a daydream. You might be staring at a tumbling leaf when a bolt of inspiration hits. Sometimes, no matter where you are, what you need for a poem or story will sprint out to find you. If you're a creative writer, your Muse will tend to visit when you carve out time to fool around with words. Your Muse isn't interested in whether you print or prefer cursive. She doesn't care if you misspell words or make incomplete or run-on sentence "mistakes." Your Muse just wants to communicate to *that part of you* who's open to believing and can risk *feeling*. Sometimes I imagine my Muse as a guide who wears a glow-in-the-dark gown. Like a great spark, she passes through the gates of my imagination, leaving images in the shape of fireflies, that guide me into unknown territory.

What does your Muse look like? If you're not sure, ask him or her. . . . No two Muses are alike. Here two young writers describe their Muse.

He's very strong, like a golden flicker of light. He has glittering eyes like rubies and trusts competition. He's as strong as an African crocodile. His voice is filled with soothing wisdom. Though he looks fierce on the outside, on the inside he's sweet and kind-hearted. When he feels like it, he can cradle the world in his arms.

—Sam

She is kind and forgiving. Kept in a pink glass bottle, she is taken out when needed. Like a winding path to happiness, she whispers, and can melt right down then grow back into life again. She is a fragment of peace and happiness, yet has her own style with neat little feet and silky brown hair. She wears rings of hope and ear-rings of love. She is like a blue and purple cloud . . . a clear sky with only one star.

—Chloe

Dear Fellow Writer,

I've received a lot of great advice from other writers, so I wanted to share my favorite piece of advice with you. The amazing Ray Bradbury (*Dandelion Wine, The Halloween Tree, Something Wicked This Way Comes,* etc.) once told me that writers should always eat sandwiches for lunch. I didn't understand at first (although it sounded yummy). He explained that if you had a sandwich for lunch, it was easier to read and eat at the same time. Bradbury knew, as most writers do, that reading is as important to the growth of a writer as writing is. Writers should be reading all the time; it's the best way to learn how to write.

Read a lot, and read all kinds of books. And when people give you a hard time because you're reading, tell them you're busy working.

Best wishes,

Lewis Buzbee

A Sample of Lewis Buzbee's Writing

FROM *Steinbeck's Ghost*

Travis looked at the stacks of books on his desk. These were his new life, his real life. *A Wrinkle in Time* led him to the library. Which led him to *Corral de Tierra*, which led him to *The Pastures of Heaven*, which led him to *The Long Valley*. And these books led him to the other mysteries that surrounded him—Gitano and the Dark Watchers and Steinbeck's ghost—led him deeper into a world he'd never suspected. Books could do that to you. When you read, the world really did change. He understood this now. You saw parts of the world you never knew existed. Books were in the world; the world was in books.

Lewis Buzbee has written several books for adults, but much prefers to write for kids, because they're a lot smarter. He is the author of Steinbeck's Ghost, The Haunting of Charles Dickens, *and is working on* Mark Twain and the Mysterious Stranger.

A New Recipe

When I was your age, my mom made breakfast and packed my lunch pail while my dad got ready for work, and my nana—who lived down the street—sat at our kitchen table, reading the newspaper, even though the headlines made her sad. One morning, my 3-year-old sister came running down the hall from the direction of my bedroom, saying *uh oh*—and I knew something important had been ruined. *It's OK—things break; things spill,* my mom sighed, removing what was mine from my sister's clenched fists. Feeling invisible, I slid into my chair, picked up a spoon and looked from my cereal bowl out the back window, where rain was beginning to fall on the bicycle I'd left in the weeds, next to a sweater in a damp heap. It was a gray day, and I was on my way into a poor-me funk when Nana looked over and winked at me. That was all the inspiration I needed to borrow rain from the nearest cloud and the point from a far-off star. Sitting there, daydreaming, I combined the scent of a flower, a dash of early morning, and 3 handfuls of the daring it took for my sister to touch something in *my* room. I shredded 7 ounces of doubt, stirred in a small pout and, with a magical chant, whipped my disappointment into a day of stormy excitement with a rainbow of understanding placed way up on top.

Have you ever felt invisible and wished for your day to be different in some big or small way? Have you ever wanted to make something broken by curious hands, or ruined by rain, brand new again? Your imagination is long and tireless. Let the surface of a real-life story you'd like to change spin in a new direction. Just by changing your mind, your heart can cast a spell of wonder over *anything*. Choose a few ingredients from your imagination or borrow some from Mother Nature to make a new color, a recipe for a friendship, even a gray, rainy morning into a rainbow . . . all because of a little wink.

Your Turn

Measuring Sound, Mixing Feeling

Go on, measure out a few cups of a blue jay's *caw,* sprinkle in a teaspoon of courage; stir up a handful of humming, crack open a scream. Whip up a poetry sandwich with a side of pride and then nibble on the darkest words you've ever heard. Measure anything you think you can't touch or reach, set the timer, and find out what it takes to be a writer-baker in this kooky cooking school called life.

4 cups of   a pinch of   a heaping tablespoon of

drizzle in   splatter   teaspoon

          ladel   frost with   dash   fold in

sprinkle   stir   taste   sift

          a basket of   mix   pour

add   beat   handful

213

whisk together   a day's worth   crack open

half an hour of   broil   measure out   let boil

bake for   a bunch of   freeze

cool   defrost   scramble   cook

twist   thaw   add a pinch

heat   palmful   ocean's worth

simmer   combine   a pint of

a slice of   grate   chop   mash

puree   toss   blanch   blend

sprinkle   thimble's worth   crush up

shake in   a year's supply of   a day's worh

350 degrees   a lifetime of   borrow some

Recipe for Peace

Ingredients: 2 cups inspiration. 1 quart imagination. 3 tablespoons wonder. 1 teaspoon metaphor. Enough time to bake thoroughly. Mix in a large bowl, 50 strokes. Add a pinch of love to taste. Generously sprinkle in wonder; fold in eagerness. Bake for 30 years at high degrees. Don't worry if toothpick comes out moist. Let cool on a windowsill, facing east. Light a candle. Serve the world.

—Carly

Try This. . . . .

Show Don't Tell

Pick your favorite color and then describe it *without* mentioning it anywhere in your writing. Don't breathe a word of it, not even in your title. Go ahead, write about the closest thing your color reminds you of, tastes and smells of, something that hangs in your closet that's this color, things found in nature that hold its hue, where it shimmers, what makes it glimmer. . . . Mention shapes and sounds, offer curved hints and slanted clues. Just don't mention white, green, orange, brown, or blue. You can also include what *isn't* your color. As you write, don't worry too much. (Worry has a way of seeping in and ruining your writing.) Trust your poem enough to be fun and true for *you*.

When you're done, read what you wrote to a friend and see if she can guess what color you're describing. Ask your friend for the tip-off image that made him guess the color he said. Then use *this* line for your title.

It shimmers through my curtains
where my window shines.
On my porch gardenias bloom.
I've never seen the moon
when the clinging breath
of the sky blankets the universe.
My great-grandma's plates
gleam with their golden
trim and violet swirls.
Even the dark earth
holds it against the air above.
A lacy communion dress
hangs in my sister's closet.
Skulls of sugar cane sell
on the day of the dead.

—Becky

(Tip-off image: "Even the dark earth
holds it against the air above.")
(Answer: White)

The sliding of yesterday
and the power of the fields.
Not the life of sadness,
but the joy of wisdom.
and cracks of wind.
Not stuck inside a black box,
but the rapids in a river—
with the fish all going upstream:
swish swish swish.
The sparks of starlight
And the heart of the sky.

—Shay

(Tip-off image: "the heart of the sky.")
(Answer: Blue)

Your Turn

Concrete Poems

Concrete poems are written in the shape of what they are. Not-too-complicated shapes work best. You might write that poem about the kid who wanted to be king in the shape of a crown. When your grandma beats you at tennis, scribble your rant in the shape of a racquet. A wave for that boogie board wipeout on Sandy's Beach. The full-moon for the poem about your favorite camping trip. A single leaf for your ode to autumn. You can even cover the page in one slanted word— "r-a-i-n"—over and over again. (This is called a calligram.) Other easy ideas for concrete poems: a pencil, door, house, pyramid, hand, fence, tree, boat, candle, fish, and the head of your tough-talking cat.

All the Places That Feel Like Home

Up
in the trees,
all kinds except the
ones that don't have branches.
In my bedroom, on a plane, in the outback
of Australia. At a party, at my grandma's, down by the creek.
At the lake, but only with people
I know. Home is in my bed with
my mom and dad, or outside in
the backyard when it's raining.
Or in the snow. Or upstairs eating
Rice Chex Cereal. Home is late at night
when I'm listening to the crickets
as my
hamster
runs on
his little
exercise
wheel.

—Group poem

Rip the Page!

Get your hands on an encyclopedia of reptiles and write down as many names of any and all scaly things that creep you out, terrify, or amaze you. Cut the page into slithering shapes. Fill each shape with these side-winding snake and leaping-lizard names, including where they live in the world, how they sleep, who they like to bite, poison, swallow, and eat. Find the one you'll keep as a pet and let the rest roam free. (Just keep them away from me!)

Mule Fog With a Chance Of Grasshopper Rain

Mentioning the weather in your writing can deepen the mood of what you're saying in an unexpected way . . . and adding an animal or reptile to your writing can lend a furry or scaly friendliness to your poem or story, while letting your reader experience the great outdoors in a whole new way. Draw lines and arrows to mix and match animals and types of weather in the list below. Become a zany weatherkid and forecast a day or an entire season's weather in the first two lines of a poem. *Look for an elk avalanche this weekend with a slight chance of stampeding zebra.* Or maybe write about what happens when the weather runs away, as it did in this example:

As the fire is burning up on the hill, it does a little shimmy and dances like dogs. Each breath the garden takes circles above, sending flowers off into the night. The snow roams wherever you take it and lightning flares pointing its index finger. Thunder escapes from its deathly hollow, drives up in its weather mobile and scares away the grizzly bears.

—Maddie

Or you might want to write about what happens when animals take on the qualities of the weather.

That was the year the iguanas grew feet made out of sleet and the lemurs' tails became mudslides of shadow and snow. Sure, it got cold, even the apple moths' wings started to resemble icicles flecked with lightning . . . as they flew north, south, east, west, in search of another route home.

lemur	rain	iguana	snow
wind	mule	sleet	shadows
shady	glacier	northerly	mud slide
apple moth	tornado	rabbit	hurricane
jet stream	wolverine	sunshine	bobcat
iced-over	downpour	drifts	cloud cover
drizzle	coyote	blizzard	giant cockroach
weevils	trade winds	humid	flood
black widow	millipede	peacock	miles an hour
fog	coyote	jackrabbit	lobster
melting	volcanic	flow	windchill
lightning	thunder	polar bear	piranha
sweltering	scarlet macaw	ice crystals	zebra
howling	salmon	minnows	westerly
drought	giraffe	dragonfly	ostrich
gorilla	gecko	tsunami	armadillo
frost	fleas	temperature	precipitation
degrees	avalanche	tropical	twister

Dear _____,

Sometimes you have to let your poem lead you. Even though you may find it going in a completely different direction. Don't worry. Let it go and follow it there. Are you afraid of something? Do you wonder why about something? Write about it. Let yourself write *without* thinking. Make yourself keep writing. This lets you go deeper and deeper and lets you get closer and closer to the truths you hold guarded. Putting words together into a poem is like working a jigsaw puzzle. Every word should need to be there: for meaning, for rhythm, for originality, for self-discovery, and for connection. It's a great adventure, writing poems. Have at it. And don't forget to have fun. Someday I hope to read what you've written.

Best wishes,

Lyn (C. B. Follett)

A Sample of C. B. Follett's Writing

Hopscotch

I had the perfect pebble,
almost a square
a rounded pillow of a square
and it was cream-colored

with a green line
that ran across in one direction
and a black line
that crossed it the other way
like an Xmas present.

I kept it in my pocket
rubbing it for luck before a math test
or before making the first toss
into the eight squares
drawn on the playground.

In those days
I could balance on one leg
like a heron in a swift moving stream.
I could bend
as in ballet and pause
above the pebble,
pick it up delicate as a mule
nibbles grass,
unwind, and hop on my way.

I was so good at hopscotch,
the other girls began to eye
my magical pebble as the source.
They made up rules such as—
winner gets to choose a pebble, or

no pebbles with stripes.

C. B. Follett—or 'Lyn, as her friends call her—is an artist and a poet who has won some awards and been nominated for five Pushcart Prizes. Her most recent book is And Freddy Was My Darling *(Many Voices Press, 2009) named after a boy she knew since kindergarten.*

The Editing Mouse

There are some words you just *don't* need to keep in your poems and stories. When your writing is too full, *that's* the time to bring out the Editing Mouse, to eat up the extra words. Sometimes by reading what you've written *out loud* to the walls, windows, posts, and beams, your voice will give you clues about the words you must feed to the Editing Mouse. Some days the editing mouse is especially hungry. Some days writing is about re-writing, crossing out words and adding others. If something doesn't work in your poem or story on a Monday, but you *really, really* love it . . . save it for a new poem or story you begin on Tuesday. Kind of like the way your mom wraps up leftover chicken to be used later in the week for a salad or a casserole. Let's face it, sometimes one extra word can drag a whole poem or story

d
  o

    w
      n.

Just as you clear your throat before you speak to get to the clear voice underneath, the first part of your writing is sometimes like a cough. You don't need those words. They were only necessary to get you to the real beginning—*not* what you want to have sit on the page *forever.* This advice works for the last part of your writing, too, especially if you've summed everything up for your reader and left no room for anyone (including yourself) to be surprised. You *must* be bold enough to cut out the parts in your writing where you've told too much and left nothing for your reader to discover on their own. The Editing Mouse likes to be fed everything on the page that tells too much and doesn't sound right; everything you trip over when you read your writing out loud; all the not-quite-right words you might like but just don't need. That said, there are times when you want to write (and write) and share everything, all your hopes, dreams, extra words, and feelings, with no one but *me, myself, and I.* You don't want to let the Editing Mouse out. You don't even like mice. In which case, this writer says, *fine.*

Try This....

Picture Your Closest Friend

Who's the friend you can do absolutely nothing with and still have a blast? The friend you can't wait to see again, even after spending an entire afternoon sitting in the shade, eating grapes. You know all about her zany imagination, and the look her face makes before she laughs; you can imitate his walk and mimic his goofy talk. So why not sit down and dash off a mini-portrait? Fool around with metaphors and similes to describe your friend's hair and eyes, cheeks and teeth. The next time you meet to eat grapes, ask your friend if she'd like to *read* one of your favorite photographs.

Sasha

Her hair is like calm waves pushing against the sand. When she blinks, it's like pink-white-yellow flowers opening and closing. Her eyelashes are like black needles that keep sewing and sewing. Her imagination flashes like lightning. When she walks, her footsteps sound like the wind blowing the trees. Her lips are glossy and beam like fire. Her fingers are soft and scaly like snakes. Her ears are oval and hollow like tunnels. Her teeth are clear diamonds lighting a cave. Her cheeks are like little pads of butter. When she touches me, I feel warm and safe—like I want to *whoosh* down a waterfall.

—Livie

227

My Best Friend

His brain is Albert Einstein.
His heart, a singing dream.
His legs, a trampling horse.
His mouth, a cave
with icicles hanging down.

—Robbie

Your Turn

Suddenly a Story....

Your Favorite Age

With the help of hundreds of photos—taken by my Grandma Betty—I can honestly say I loved being a baby. Here I am sitting in the kitchen cupboard, wearing a green plastic bowl for a hat . . . in this one, I'm standing on a mound of sand with my cats, Crooked Tail and Sam-I-Am. I remember discovering the magic of words, the afternoon I put *please may I have a* before *c-o-o-k-i-e* and got it; the freedom that came at 5 when I learned how to roller skate; and the day Jimmy Ferguson, who sat across from me in first grade, dared me to taste the paste. With my friend Cathy Jolley I hung upside down from the jungle gym at recess and lost my milk money in the grass. There was the smell of tanbark and the clanging sound of the monkey rings I loved to swing on, never mind the sting of blisters rising across my hands. I played Catch and Count Down and Keep Away From the Cootie Kissers, the yard duty's whistle reminding me it was time to line up to go inside. Looking back, I watch my life ripple and unwind through a hop-scotch of space and time, with me in the center of all that swirling light, climbing the steps yet again to race down the silver slide.

Can you bring some of your earliest memories back to life on the page? Flip through a photo album and find a few, listen to your favorite music, or simply record what you see behind your eyelids as you let some memories float up to find you.

Your Turn

Rip the Page!

Do you ever imagine who you'll be in the future? Write a letter to that person who will be you one day. Include what you imagine you'll look like, what your job will be, a description of the house you'll live in. Include something about who you are now, at this exact moment in time: what you ate for breakfast, the names of your friends, where you're sitting as you write this, what you're thinking about, what's going on in the next room. Then stuff this page into an envelope, address it to yourself, find a stamp, and ask your mom or dad to mail it in ten or twenty years. Then forget about it. Maybe it will arrive one day when you least expect it and most need to read it.

P.S. KEEP FLEXING

It's been 232 pages since we first met, and you now have an invisible muscle to flex—that has *nothing* to do with lifting weights. And *nothing* to do with grades, gold stars, or glowing report cards. You can't see this muscle in the bathroom mirror. You can't measure it by lifting up a car or earn it by memorizing facts. That's because this muscle has *everything* to do with the way you *pay attention* to your mysterious, sweet, confusing, fun-filled life of deep-swirling ideas, thoughts, daydreams, and feelings. It's a muscle that grows in strength the more you play the game of meeting your curiosity on (and off) the page, and greeting all the words, images, scraps of dialogue, and broken bits of truth (whatever *your* truth is to *you*) of everything you love and understand, *and* everything you don't yet and can't yet love and understand. Letter by wobbly letter, this muscle might quiver at times as you cross the vast distances of your imagination's wild wanderings, but by now you know that this quiver, too, is part of the journey.

The more you use and trust this creative muscle, the more alive to *everything* you become, and the more its brightness can shine out for your friends, your family, and the world to see. It's sort of like an equation that equals how much you believe in the wisdom of your heart + how much you're willing to reveal (and be surprised by) the one-of-a-kind being that you are. And then, of course, how much of this equation you can get on to the page.

So enjoy it all—the walk, the run, the skip, the glide, even the occasional tumble and fall of this adventure that begins (again and again) the instant you pick up a pen.

To Continue the Writing Adventure

If you'd like to experiment with the Try This writing prompts, poems, and Suddenly a Story . . . . ideas presented in this book, I love to visit classrooms, libraries, and book fairs to play on the page with kids and kids-at-heart. Simply write to me and include your name, an adult's name, snail mail, and e-mail addresses and one of the writing experiments you like best. I look forward to hearing from you!

To share your writing with magazines that publish the work of creative kids, here's a short list to get you started:

KidSpirit magazine is for young people (11–15 years old) of all backgrounds who like to think about "the meaning of life and the big questions that affect us all." Kidspirit Magazine, 77 State Street, Brooklyn, NY 11201 or visit www.kidspiritmagazine.com

"The Children's Corner" of *The Louisville Review* accepts poetry from students in grades K–12. They seek writing that looks for fresh ways to recreate scenes and feelings. The Louisville Review 851 S. Fourth St., Louisville, KY 40203 or email: louisvillereview@spalding.edu

Magic Dragon publishes poems, stories, and essays by children in elementary school and encourages kids to be "unafraid to express their creative ideas so they can grow to be adults unafraid to apply a creative approach to their lives and word." Magic Dragon, P.O. Box 687, Webster, NY 14580 or visit www.magicdragonmagazine.com

My Hero is an internet archive of hero stories from around the world for all ages. It hosts thousands of stories of remarkable people written by children and adults alike. Tell the world about your hero. The My Hero Project, 1278 Glenneyre #286, Laguna Beach, CA 92651. www.myhero.com

New Moon is the "Magazine for Girls and Their Dreams" (sorry, boys!) and is for girls ages 8–14. New Moon, 34 East Superior St., #200, Duluth, MN 55802. www.newmoon.org

River of Words sponsors an annual poetry and art contest for students. www.riverofwords.org

Skipping Stones publishes letters, riddles, personal-experience essays, and short stories by children ages 8–16. Skipping Stones, P.O. Box 3939, Eugene, OR 97403. www.skipping-stones.org

Stone Soup publishes poems and stories by kids through age 13. www.stonesoup.com

ACKNOWLEDGMENTS

My thanks to the children who inspired this book by sharing their secrets of creativity and to the teachers who welcome me into their classrooms, especially those who pick up a pen and write with their students.

Big love to Owen and Collin, and to Nina Nelson, Marlene Benke, Brian Lewis, Dawn Antonelli, and Alison Altmann for always being in my corner.

Thanks to my friends for cheering me on, especially Joan Kip, Lynn Mundell, Courtney and Marco della Cava, Mary Lea Crawley, Michelle Lester, and James Higgins.

Stacks of appreciation to Yolanda Fletcher, Head Children's Librarian at the Mill Valley Public Library, and to Naima Dean, Katie MacBride, Kathy Wilhelm, and Shannon Jones.

A deep bow to my teachers, past and present, Jane Hirshfield, Anne Barrows, Gary Thompson, Natalie Goldberg, and Francesca McCartney for shining their light on my path.

Gratitude to every note-giver and excerpt-loaner who took time away from their own projects to offer me a contribution: Avi, Annie Barrows, Lewis Buzbee, Cathy Carmadelle, Lucille Clifton, Karen Cushman, Carol Edgarian, Moira Egan, Kathy Evans, Betsy Franco, 'Lyn Follett, Grace Marie Grafton, Daniel Handler, Paul Hoover, Elizabeth Singer Hunt, C. M. Mayo, Naomi Shihab Nye, Patricia Polacco, Gary Soto, Linda Wolfe, Susan Wooldridge, and my dear friend, Prartho Sereno, who inspires me to discover my heart's true abundance and who, along with my fellow poet-teachers in the California Poets in the Schools program, shared lesson plan gems.

High fives to Trisha Garlock, KIDDO, and The Marin Community Foundation for funding poetry in the schools; and to the Marin Arts Council Fund for Artists for awarding me a much-needed grant.

Thank you to my agent, Stefanie Von Borstal and Full Circle Literary for introducing me to the creative team at Shambhala Publications/Roost Books. This book is much better because of assistant editor Chloe Foster's eagle eyes; book designer Lora Zorian's flair with font size and a certain shade of blue; publicist Jennifer Campaniolo's understanding about summertime travel plans; and Jennifer Urban-Brown's praise, patience, and professionalism. I couldn't have dreamed up a better editor to guide *Rip the Page!* to completion.

"Read like a wolf eats."
—*Gary Paulsen*

Here are some books that inspired me while I wrote Rip the Page!

Alice's Adventures in Wonderland and *Through the Looking Glass* by Lewis Carroll

The Book of Light by Lucille Clifton

The Book of Qualities by J. Ruth Gendler

The Book of Questions (translated by William O'Daly), *Odes to Common Things,* and *Odes to Opposites* by Pablo Neruda

A Brief History of Punctuation: Poems by Maurya Simon

Call from Paris and *Everyday Miracles* by Prartho Sereno

Children's Miscellany: Useless Information That's Essential to Know and *Children's Miscellany Too: More Useless Information That's Essential to Know* by Matthew Morgan and Samantha Barnes

Finding What You Didn't Lose: Expressing Your Truth and Creativity through Poem-Making by John Fox

A Fire in My Hands: A Book of Poems by Gary Soto

Foolsgold: Making Something from Nothing and Freeing Your Creative Process and *poemcrazy: Freeing Your Life with Words* by Susan G. Wooldridge

Given Words by Elizabeth White

Haiku Mind: 108 Poems to Cultivate Awareness and Open Your Heart by Patricia Donegan

How to Be an Explorer of the World: Portable Life Museum and *Wreck this Journal* by Keri Smith

How to Haiku: A Writer's Guide to Haiku and Related Forms by Bruce Ross

I Never Told Anybody: Teaching Poetry Writing to Old People and *Making Your Own Days: The Pleasures of Reading and Writing Poetry* by Kenneth Koch

If You Want To Write: A Book about Art, Independence, and Spirit by Brenda Ueland

If You're Afraid of the Dark, Remember the Night Rainbow by Cooper Edens

The Invisible Ladder: An Anthology of Contemporary American Poems for Young Readers, edited by Liz Rosenberg

Never in a Hurry: Essays on People and Places by Naomi Shihab Nye

One Continuous Mistake: Four Noble Truths for Writers and *Writing the Fire! Yoga and the Art of Making Your Words Come Alive* by Gail Sher

Poetry in Motion: 100 Poems from the Subways and Buses, edited by Molly Peacock, Elise Paschen, and Neil Neches

Quote Poet Unquote: Contemporary Quotations on Poets and Poetry, edited by Dennis O'Driscoll

Riddles: Knowledge Cards by Emmanuel Williams

Runny Babbit, A Billy Sook by Shel Silverstein

The Teachers and Writers Handbook of Poetic Forms by Ron Padgett

The Triggering Town: Lectures and Essays on Poetry and Writing by Richard Hugo

Unleashed: Poems by Writers' Dogs, edited by Amy Hempel and Jim Shepard

Walking on Alligators: A Book of Meditations for Writers by Susan Shaughnessy

Wonderful Words, Silent Truth: Essays on Poetry and a Memoir by Charles Simic

Writing Down the Bones: Freeing the Writer Within by Natalie Goldberg

Writing Toward Home: Tales and Lessons to Find Your Way by Georgia Heard

Here are some books I can wholeheartedly recommend

11 Birthdays, Jeremy Fink and the Meaning of Life, and *A Mango-Shaped Space* by Wendy Mass

The Adventures of Tim by Edward Ardizzone

Basho and the Fox by Tim Myers

The Big Bazoohley by Peter Carey

Carbonel: The King of Cats by Barbara Sleigh

Causing A Stir: The Secret Lives and Loves of Kitchen Utensils by Prartho Sereno

Charlotte's Web and *Stuart Little* by E. B. White

Confetti Girl by Diana Lopez

A Curious Collection of Cats: Concrete Poems and *Mathematickles!* by Betsy Franco

Danny the Champion of the World and *The Enormous Crocodile* by Roald Dahl

Ereth's Birthday, Poppy, Poppy and Rye, and *Ragweed* by Avi

Frindle, No Talking, and *The School Story* by Andrew Clements

From the Mixed-Up Files of Mrs. Basil E. Frankweiler by E. L. Konigsburg

God Went to Beauty School, Gooseberry Park, The Old Lady Who Named Things, and *The Van Gough Café* by Cynthia Rylant

Granny Torrelli Makes Soup, Hate That Cat: A Novel, and *Love That Dog: A Novel* by Sharon Creech

The Graves Family, The Graves Family Goes Camping, Mrs. Mack, Pink and Say, and *Thank You, Mr. Falker* by Patricia Polacco

Grrrrr: A Collection of Poems about Bears, edited by C. B. Follett

The House on Mango Street by Sandra Cisneros

Illuminations: Great Writers on Writing, edited by Christina Davis and Christopher Edgar

Iris and Walter series by Elissa Haden Guest

Ivy + Bean and *The Magic Half* by Annie Barrows

Lemony Snicket's A Series of Unfortunate Events by Lemony Snicket

Love, Ruby Lavender by Deborah Wiles

The Magic Treehouse series by Mary Pope Osborne

Mandy and *The Last of the Really Great Whangdoodles* by Julie Andrews Edwards

The Miraculous Journey of Edward Tulane by Kate DiCamillo

The Mouse and The Motorcycle by Beverly Cleary

Neighborhood Odes: A Poetry Collection by Gary Soto

No Flying in the House by Betty Brock

Oh Yuck! The Encyclopedia of Everything Nasty by Joy Masoff

The Penderwicks: A Summer Tale of Four Sisters, Two Rabbits, and a Very Interesting Boy and *The Penderwicks on Gardam Street* by Jeanne Birdsall

Seeing the Blue in Between: Advice and Inspiration for Young Poets by Paul B. Janeczko

Steinbeck's Ghost by Lewis Buzbee

Stories of the Poets by Suzi Mee

Tales From Outer Suburbia by Shaun Tan

Tales of a Fourth Grade Nothing by Judy Blume

This Is Just to Say: Poems of Apology and Forgiveness by Joyce Sidman

This Same Sky: A Collection of Poems from Around the World, edited by Naomi Shihab Nye

Weslandia by Paul Fleischman

When You Teach Me by Rebecca Stead

A Wrinkle in Time by Madeleine L'Engle

INDEX OF WRITING EXPERIMENTS

Michelle Lester

Karen Benke has inspired children in the art of creative writing for sixteen years as a writing coach, free-write facilitator, and poet-teacher in the California Poets in the Schools program, where she specializes in leading workshops for children in elementary and middle schools. The author of a chapbook of poems, *Sister* (Prescott, Ariz.: Conflux Press, 2004), she completed her MA in Writing from the University of San Francisco and her BA in English from California State University, Chico. The recipient of a teaching grant from Poets & Writers, Inc., and a four-time grant recipient from the Marin Arts Council Fund for Artists, she lives with her family in Mill Valley, California. Visit her website at www.karenbenke.com.

246